FINDING THE INNOVATION GAP

Finding The Innovation Gap:

Disruptive idea, A better way of managing prototypes

Baisham Chatterjee

iUniverse, Inc.
New York Bloomington

Finding the innovation gap:
Disruptive idea, A better way of managing prototypes

Copyright © 2010 by Baisham Chatterjee

All rights reserved. No part of this book may be used or reproduced by any means, graphic, electronic, or mechanical, including photocopying, recording, taping or by any information storage retrieval system without the written permission of the publisher except in the case of brief quotations embodied in critical articles and reviews.

The views expressed in this work are solely those of the author and do not necessarily reflect the views of the publisher, and the publisher hereby disclaims any responsibility for them.

iUniverse books may be ordered through booksellers or by contacting:

iUniverse
1663 Liberty Drive
Bloomington, IN 47403
www.iuniverse.com
1-800-Authors (1-800-288-4677)

Because of the dynamic nature of the Internet, any Web addresses or links contained in this book may have changed since publication and may no longer be valid.

ISBN: 978-1-4502-0320-3 (sc)
ISBN: 978-1-4502-0321-0 (ebk)

Printed in the United States of America

iUniverse rev. date: 12/21/2009

Author Biography

I have started my career around 3 and a half years back from a massive project at PANalytical(Spectris technologies). After that I took up the marketing of a German firm and started contributing through a massive blog. I took admission at UNBSJ on October 6th 2008. After that I wrote papers on corporate strategy, business research, HR, E-commerce and did a breakthrough project at Propelsj. I have another blog site as mf66 on ideablob.com (the firm recently went bankrupt). I now blog on Propelsjs provincial business development site. I also have huge paper reports posted at Ivey Business Journal. I recently wrote a book Reconstructing Competition and its processes also published at iUniverse.

Acknowledgements

First of all I thank my father Dr Sanat Kumar Chatterjee from whom I learnt that I have to contribute. He has written many papers for American Journals in material sciences and has earlier written 2 books on material sciences for **Prentice Hall of India** and **Springer Verlag** (both on X-Ray Crystallography). He helped me prepare the diagrams in the computer format from the hand sketched diagrams that I prepared. I also thank Stephen Bernhut (editor Ivey Business Journal) for recognizing my views on the paper reports that I post at Ivey. I also thank Prof Gregory Fleet for having given me the base to contribute further. I also thank Jeff Roach of Propelsj for giving me the opportunity to take up a project work in his business as well as contribute on his provincial business development site. I also thank Roger Moser (Prof EBS), Mark Hollingworth (Prof McGill and author of the book **Growing people Growing Companies)** and Martijn J Fransen (PANalytical) for helping me with my progress. I also thank Ann Marie Stephen, Bonnie Sudul and Meredith Joy Henry for helping me with the progress regarding my classes in the university and my book. I sincerely thank John Potts and Eric Hanselmann of iUniverse for helping me publish my book.

Preface and introduction.

I named my book **Finding the innovation gap: Disruptive idea, A better way of managing prototypes** because of the high impact of innovative ideas in the modern world and the recent impact and the necessity of performance in modern business. Impact seems to be a key focus that is adjoined to alliances and organizational and locational performance to help in giving a key figure to performance in the modern world. The chapters are organized as:

Chapter1consists of the basis of innovation that consists of the basic ideas which are the core processes of modern businesses and ideas that have spurred the major idealistic phenomenon of innovation around 10 years back which brought the new images in innovation from where the other ideas like high impact businesses, alliances in innovation and OI took a major form and focus.

Chapter2 consists of increasing effectiveness by using economics of innovation, where the success is from resource utilization, human resource analysis, technology usage, as well as look at technical appropriability, process, costs, salesforce development and utilization of the most certain parts of an economy.

Chapter3 consists of ideas starting from describing innovation to understanding the organizational impact. The major role in this plays with Canadian businesses, R&Ds, IPRs, performance innovation, TMT development styles and different organizational strategies as from the work of Richard E. Caves and Michael E. Porter.

Chapter4 deals with developing on the locational theory and performance management. It consists of different challenges like Webers theory and Hoovers cost factor location and ideas from Thunen-Weber type of theory and return on management. Kaplan&Nortons balanced scorecard for improving performance is another field to deal with.

Chapter5 deals with how integrated companies find a secure knowhow base and work on that. Their various ideas start with key account management. Customer design, key product design specifications, customer feedback system and flexible manufacturing system are the important ideas to deal with.

Chapter6 talks of management techniques for managing innovation and this is a chapter which forms a supportive base in the middle to help the other chapters or provide foundation to the other chapters. In this chapter I talk of the focus of RAND Corporation, NRC-IRAP and help prepare a research framework and licensing of a product.

Chapter7 depends on ideas by Clayton Christensen and my own ideas on disruptive technology. All the models are self-created through my personal understanding of disruptive technology and my own concepts added through the analytical understanding.

Chapter8 consists of a large set of data collected from different journals and articles to make a very different analysis on sustaining and disruptive technologies. This chapter consists of modern firms and economies that depend on this idea as well as putting further emphasis on emerging and converging technologies as well as the S-curve, and making an analysis of the most advanced disruptive ideas.

Chapter9 covers ideas on alliances in innovation for product development, where different structures has been brought to view , like Mobides action plans and strategic alliances, competitive landscape, other factors involved are value proposition and R&D collaborators.

Chapter10 covers high impact businesses: providing vision and control that depends on a lot of ideas starting from analysis of high impact businesses and why they have been so successful.

Chapter11starts from generalizations of observations and R&D innovation cycles, effective R&D and relative ideas, as well as understand the dilemmas and classifications of R&D. There are also ways of understand the ways of bringing together obsolete technology and working on that.

Chapter12 covers an idea of prototype management by measuring prototype products in ICT firms as well as telecommunications. It is important to understand integrated technologies and systems, key production costs, problem solving systems as well as bringing in rapid prototyping and dimensional prototype models as well as virtual prototyping.

Conclusion is an analysis and suggestions of why my work is so important and carries great advantage in the modern innovation and technology perspective with most of the ideas being totally involved in the orientation of a new business concept formula. The data is very original and fluent to give better and sharper outlook.

Contents

Author Biography   v
Acknowledgements   vii
Preface and introduction.   ix

1: BASIC MINDSET OF INNOVATION   1
2: INCREASING EFFECTIVENESS BY USING ECONOMICS TO INNOVATION   12
3: DESCRIBING INNOVATION AND ORGANIZATIONAL IMPACT   22
4: DEVELOPING ON THE LOCATIONAL THEORY AND PERFORMANCE MANAGEMENT   34
5: INTEGRATED COMPANIES: HOW THEY WORK   43
6: MANAGEMENT TECHNIQUES FOR MANAGING INNOVATION   51
7: DIFFERENT FACTORS TO FIND THE INNOVATION GAP AND IMPROVE ON IT   60
8: FURTHER ANALYSIS ON SUSTAINING AND DISRUPTIVE TECHNOLOGIES   73
9: ALLIANCES IN INNOVATION FOR PRODUCT DEVELOPMENT   84
10: HIGH IMPACT BUSINESSES: PROVIDING VISION AND FOCUS   97
11: MODERN IMPLICATIONS ON RESEARCH AND DEVELOPMENT   110
12: PROTOTYPE MANAGEMENT   122
13: CONCLUSION   130

References   135

Chapter 1

(Baisham Chatterjee student UNBSJ)
Basic mindset of innovation

Product innovation provides the most obvious means of generating revenues whereas process innovation helps in improving quality and also for saving costs. All respected organizations have a set of core products that evaluates the power that other products can gain, and evaluates, buying and using core products. This makes the products as well as the firms competitive position indisputable. Productivity gains offers the same performance at lower costs and develop newer products. Market segmentation helps in dividing a total potential market into smaller more manageable parts which helps in developing profitability of a business. Core product features consist of differentiated features, undifferentiated features which consists of the major challenges for developing on them like: system-buy, consulting and commodity.

It is very necessary to combine innovation to the limitations of a business. The innovative abilities are like managing change at an operational level and provide training. Look forward towards cost control and culture that builds entrepreneurship and employee empowerment as well as develop cost effective solutions to help in exploiting new technologies, co-ordinate global strategy and look at the market potentiality. It is said that innovation is positively valued by one group (marketing and

R&D) and negatively valued by another (say manufacturing). It is only then that there is intensity in strong cultures. Cultural traits is related to effectiveness and long term vision that turns out things and most important situations in understanding cultural threats and thus innovation is a serious issue to cultural response.

Innovation in products and services is related with R&D and meeting consumer needs. Innovation in management systems is usually in response to new environmental conditions, and improving the way in which people are managed and work is organized. Reengineering places large step changes that are riskier, more complex and more expensive than continuous improvement. It also places more emphasis on building improvement in its areas of operation. It has been seen that the TQM implementation comes after culture discrimination and is an important source of business innovation and is a recent area of IT communication.

Creativity sometimes leads to successful development which brings out the successful applications through the impact of innovation. Ideas are very often diverse, with different components of diverse interests and supportive management with failures being willingly tolerated and with a freedom to pursue own ideas. Moreover risk taking is encouraged, through application of adequate resources and a proper and perfect strategic direction. Strong project champion with the help of adequate funding can bring adequate funding in project. All these implications lead to successful development that can perform current products with high quality implementation. To make this process successful it is very necessary to combine different elements like customer requirements, cost information, warranty data, design guides, legal requirements, material specifications and test data.

Technological innovation process has a comparative attitude when compared to management of technology and innovation. People use different terms interchangeably when talking about the innovation process, such as: technological change, technical progress, technological development or simply innovation. Technological innovation in companies is a learning process through which a flow of new knowledge competencies and capabilities is generated. The transmission of technologies is imperfect due to multiple factors such as certain characteristics of knowledge, the existence of causal ambiguity or transaction costs. The assimilation of a new technology is not instant and depends on the level of technological knowledge previously accumulated by the company, that is to say its absorption capacity. The profits generated by a technology are not perfectly appropriable, but rather depends on the effectiveness of the protection mechanisms used by the firms.

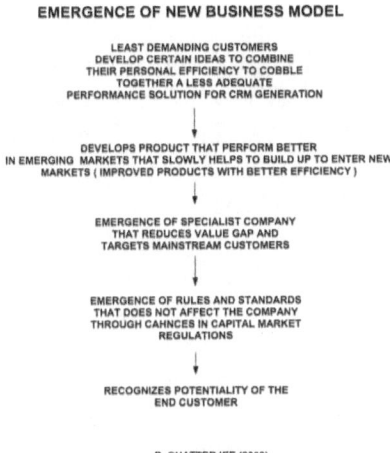

After the main material idea behind the importance and reasons for technology and innovation is completed, it is very necessary to define creativity and innovation. The steps are as idea generating by individual group, discriminating and creating a feedback loop between new and valuable idea, as well as outcome of creative behavior subjective to context specific evaluation. It is also very necessary to implement new idea that can be considered by one unit and make an assumption of the possible ideas that can be generated through the group members, who can analyze through a groupthink about prototyping and come up with ideas to reduce the effect of too many prototypes and introduce too many ideas to develop more differentiated products. Ideas behind cost analysis and multiple features and variable functioning of each feature should be analyzed. Coopers research on NPD frameworks provides a strong market orientation, an in-depth understanding of user needs and wants, a superior product with high performance to cost ratio, a strong market launch backed by significant resources devoted to selling and promotion; it is very important to have an attractive market with less skills and minimizing the risks of less product variables of an uncompetitive market. Communications is a very vulnerable area until combined with internal resource usage and marketing, which then completely makes a sense of the firms or innovators destination or product usage. There are three types of organizational competence of a solutions provider which consists of technical competence, integration competence and market/business knowledge competences that help in integrating the different departments, understand the technological prospects and thus develop a format of partnerships or a future of product development through market understanding and knowledge outlook.

We consider regulation as one of the components in the national system of innovation in which the firms develop their strategies, this strategy is related to elements such as proximity and cultural identity that allow a better perception of needs, which is crucial for the success of an innovation. Indeed the birth of innovations must generate intra-systemic interactions necessary for resolving structural tensions, the latter being not only technical but also institutional. After the structural tensions are resolved the firm brings into view the idea of new product development NPD which is a combination of certain measures like marketing database software, understanding plant equipment use which consists of automatic assembly and laser measuring to identify the main components behind production and value identification and creation. Moreover market orientation, openness to using and applying personal as well as intra firm R&D development characteristics. The other very applicable points are trusting with a main idea behind development of marketing and manufacturing capabilities. Trusting is a way of enlightenment for a business to grow further. Functional specialism and design for manufacture are the other characteristics.

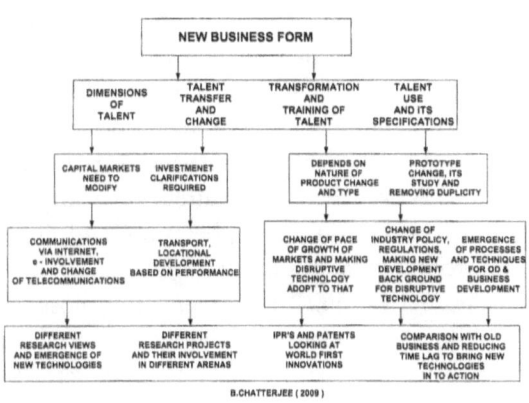

Technology consulting is another important form of innovation where the knowledge filters can impede the flow of knowledge between organizations. The factors that map and control innovation are surveillance filter, mentality filter and power filter. Surveillance filter determines the direction and scope of organizations information and mentality filter acts as a knowledge factor. It forms the existing basic assumptions of the individual. The power filter tends to filter out information that constitutes a threat to existing basic assumptions of power structures and works in favor of knowledge that strengthens ones own position. In any case of consulting innovation, the consulting unit can support product and market units through internal consulting assignments in product and business development. The surveillance filter could be observed in relation with the market units, product development and to a certain degree also product management. It is very important to commercialize these research opportunities and in order to commercialize any idea not only would they have to look at entrepreneurship, but also look at storage and re-distribution of feedback and learning through usage of various steps like opportunity recognition, research opportunity, utilization of new ideas and keep on continuously developing on it by keeping into view certain areas of control (entrepreneurial) to give a proper output. This is particularly a strategic framework and depends on few key factors dependant to change and prosper new technology where needs of society and state of art technology affect and seriously improve on the marketplace, organization and suppliers. As talked of the entrepreneurial challenge to bring this into action there is requirement of organizational support, implementation of deliberation and information access and resource configuration by use of assessment, allocation and activation. The last and the most important factor is looking at stimulation of change with idea champion, challenging norms and process facilitation being the key areas.

Innovation in different countries is termed in different ways with themes aligned to the objectives of value creation in the organization. Projects create positive changes by adding value to work processes and methods. New technologies set new standards derived from knowledge and expertise of people. Cost savings in time and manpower resources- maximizes the use of available resources. Solutions often seem to benefit other work processes and methods and become best practices in the industry. Innovation is not settling into one successful strategy, but a constant search to challenge the technologies that are at the height of success, improved results in performance arise from the search for new designs and methods that can add value to achieve phenomenal results at lower levels of cost. Looking at these key current elaborative factors on innovation, implementing a strategy for such innovation involves pursuing two basic goals: improving product/service quality with respect to two fundamental market dimensions: customers and competitors which brings out an idea of increased product competitiveness. Improving the company's technological level, once again relative to two dimensions: the current state of technological development; and competitors positioning with regard to such technologies. Consumers main priority factors in case of this is represented by performance features or simply quality and in these terms the product itself simply represents the means to achieve such functionality. It is necessary to identify a series of performance features whose effectiveness is linked to produce either the components themselves or the interrelations that provide functions. Product quality and performance features work together and share each others benefits and internal linkages to translate into the capacity gap. The specific choices of developing new markets and more advanced products and technologies are determined by a number of factors starting from different financial sets, quality, service, cost oriented results that measure the firms performance and decision making process.

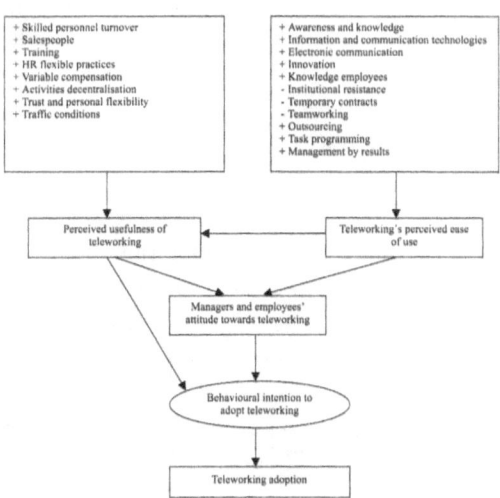

The innovation process should also be well defined through the key ideas like innovation is driven by a learning process within social groups. Customer preference, customer empowerment is very important for individuals who have a higher propensity to try innovative products than others. The speed of adoption may vary from one case to another. All these are the key elements before working up the technology S curve where the key areas of expertise are divided into three segments based on performance improvement and cumulative R and D expenditure. They are as emerging technology, developing technology and mature technology. Emerging technologies develop slowly in their early stages with performance improvement being made at a relatively high cost in time and money. But when the technology reaches a critical stage, performance improves rapidly with further expenditure, until the technology approaches its inherent limits, after which even massive expenditures will effect only marginal improvements. These marginal improvements are not only part of the expected growth, but high growth rate can be presumed by competitive responsibility and constantly rebuilding the financial assets and cost structure. The recognition of innovative opportunity will thus depend upon the recognition of limits, and on the degree of proximity to potential obsolescence. There needs to be few variety of techniques to understand the ideas behind lateral thinking, qualitative forecasting based upon Delphi or Cross-impact analysis. They help in developing existing knowledge and process capacity.

It is very often said that innovation brings forward certain tools in innovative strategies that helps in creating successful situations as well as undermine future potentialities of a business. Attack strategies, counterattack strategies and defense strategies are the key sources. Attack strategies may be used where the enterprise is in a position to gain significant competitive advantage from being the first to exploit a source of innovative opportunity. This will mean applying its existing capacity or new technology, to the marketing of new or modified products or services. Technologies that have more force to attack generally looks at penetrating into key market segments that was not observed before and thus create a position for itself. Whereas defense strategies are more related to penetrating as a means of technology and market change. Similarly counter-attack strategies are a means of effective utilization of the firms resources in order to utilize the imaginable benefits and somehow overcome excessive competition that otherwise would not have been possible. There has been very little empirical or field research available for the components and a firms overall new product strategies: it is very important to choose new markets and areas of growth and thus focus R&D efforts in different ways. This helps in understanding the level of product differential advantage and the level of product innovativeness and product concentration versus diversification. New products have a differential advantage, quality and superiority and are very often found to undergo both defensive and offensive strategies that would help target into new markets through new technological opportunities and thus improve the salary base, structure of performance for people working in the firm. Very often advertisements in magazines and journals shows their performing ability, creativity and reputation in North America. Sometimes new products are not technologically very elaborate and thought provoking this is when the business looks at more joint R&D and studies market further. This is more of a reason in developing markets which are based more on joint research and collaborations. This joint research and collaboration can be removed by:

- Technological sophistication and low budget conservative strategy can lead to higher usage of ideas and minimizing waste although location is a very important situation for this activity. Low budget conservative strategy for personal use can only be applicable for specific use in specific locations of a country.

- Similarly market newness is also very important. Moreover it is very important to undertake growth factors, market competitiveness to design a new product or enable a new product that would grow in sales volume in the new market.
- Moreover state of the art production technologies and high risk ventures are also very important to decide how to bring this new technology in the market.
- Moreover concept screening, quantification of product concept, preliminary product feasibility and development, concept testing, copy and prototype testing are very important to modify the imbalances created in any form of product understanding. These may be created at a preliminary base that doesn't require any joint research or collaboration and is possible at any location in North America or Europe with medium level skill sets.

Vertical alignment is another key form of organizational innovation which translates the business strategy's innovation objectives into an organizational strategy and an implementation plan. Horizontal alignment requires the creation of a new organizational unit or the redefinition of existing ones. Boundaries is another key important factor and when strategic partnerships fail they require to build trust, navigating different approaches to decision making, collaborating across cultures and managing communications and operations. It is not necessarily that a firm has to look at global boundaries to succeed but depend more on relationship, networking to build these qualities. Extended enterprise and internal situations are other key situations to manage.

Thus internal understanding and co-operation and understanding of defects through a perfect self measurement skills and managing future of prototypes and learning from years of experience about the market gaps and means of filling up those market gaps and creating new markets, provide the understanding of basic mindset of innovation.

A BASIC BUSINESS MODEL

B. CHATTERJEE (2009)

Chapter 2

(Baisham Chatterjee student UNBSJ) Increasing effectiveness by using economics to innovation

There are many arguments about innovation. The economic world as a whole, or some identifiable sector thereof is reasonably viewed as being in proximate equilibrium. Very certainly economic factors are dependant on choice situations and very often it is difficult to make decisions . It is difficult to choose stable choices in criteria and make its selection until the decision is completely understood and well balanced among employees. Any individual actor would could identify and would seize any available opportunity for improving outcomes and in the case of business firms would do so on pain of being eliminated by the competition of others who would identify and seize such opportunity. Any superficially stationary position involving non maximization would be altered according to the previous logic. There should be a gap between the technological innovation and a countrys economic prowess that should be recognized. The world innovation frontier helps firms in catching up to increase its rate of economic growth. The rate at which a country exploits the possibilities of a technological gap depends on the ability to mobilize resources for transforming social, institutional and economic structures. Measures of technological level and /or innovative activity may be divided into technology input measures and technology output measures. Information on scientists and engineers and their contributive ability or internal ability may be mentioned of the latter patenting activity. The patent index clearly overestimates the absolute differences in technological level between countries and R&D data which do not exist for several countries and periods.

The term technological gap has various perspectives. A very important perspective that determines it depends upon technological propensity and productivity of various nations or the comparison between where technology should go and the difference between the usage of technology and the time taken to bring out a new technology to work on.

To look at the theoretical perspective innovative technology that builds the innovation gap can be termed in three ways:

- Technology that can help a startup grow but would be difficult to be implemented in a big organization where the major challenge is reaching a wide array of customers. Few technologies prove to obtain greater importance in the long run although their area of dominance may be small or they are made more specific target oriented. These technologies are sometimes difficult to be completely utilized and improved upon without the use of particular capital intensive measures or government support. Thus the innovation gap lies in **resource utilization, time and supply chains.**
- Often there are discrepancies among countries that are producers and are the major innovators and countries that start coping up to major challenges. In this case the R&D is backed by creativity and wealth and an ability to understand the world. Whereas countries that have just started opening up their markets and economy have to make a **human resources skill analysis** and a **business environmental analysis** before making any decisions of prospering. So the difference

in developing ones core capabilities and competing with other countries depend upon these two skill sets.
- Technology usage and its key idea of being used by other firms carries a lot of statistical analysis and understanding the utilization and application of patent rights. Sometimes countries have a difficulty in understanding technology segments, various types of related technology and newly created technology. This is when an emerging country takes the advantage of their R&D and collaborations to foster development and help in creating new technology by studying used technology. The technology usage time and gap help in understanding, measuring the new technology . Only after the measurements and dimensions are created the technology development comes into action. Thus **technology usage** to create new products creates the major challenge over under analysis that can only create prototype products.
- There are also few other dimensions for development that can be carried out like entrepreneurship and studying a leaders criteria to its depth in order to formulate and understand the innovation gap. In the modern world e-online challenges and E-commerce may be used to manage this better.

There are a lot of technological gap models of economic growth that explain rather well the differences in growth between the industrialized countries as a whole in the modern world. Both the scope for imitation growth in the innovative activity and efforts to narrow the gap seem to be powerful explanatory factors of economic growth. The models are less well suited in explaining the differences in growth between developed countries, especially the small and medium sized ones most of which are on approximately the same level of development. The prospects of the group of industrialized nations would partly depend on whether or not competition through innovation will be a dominant form of competition in international markets in the future. The decreased scope for imitation which is revealed in this study and the general upturn in R&D efforts during the last years may be taken as an indication of a growing importance of technological competition in the international level.

A more general theory of economic dynamics in which diversity of technological capabilities, business strategies and expectations contribute to shape the evolutionary patterns of industries and countries. Moreover the innovation being adopted also changes over time, due to more or less incremental improvements in its performance characteristics.

It is often said that technology far from being a free good is characterized by varying degrees of appropriability of uncertainty about the technical and commercial outcomes of innovative efforts of opportunity for achieving technical advance of patterns of knowhow and hardware and of knowledge and expertise on which innovative activities are based. There are technological gaps related to different technological capabilities to innovate, different degrees of success in adopting and efficiently using product and process innovations developed elsewhere. Secondly, diversity relates to understanding the technological variety in their search procedures input combination and products even with roughly similar production costs. Thirdly it is important to understand the significant differences in the strategies of individual firms with respect to the level and composition of investment, scrapping, pricing, R&D etc.

There are very often needs for technological advancement and improvement. Economically expensive and formalized processes whose costs are measured in tables are an important function of technological advancement. Other prospects are informal processes of diffusion of information and technological capabilities. Particular forms of externalities internalized within each firm associated with learning by doing and learning by using. The adoption of innovation developed by other industries and embodied in capital equipment and intermediate inputs is also a very important source for technology development. Once the cumulative and firm-specific nature of technology is recognized, its development over time ceases to be random but is constrained to zones closely related technologically and economically related markets to existing activities. It is important to predict future patterns of innovative activities in firms, industries and countries. The technological to innovate embodied in people and firms. It is very important to note the nature of the sectoral production activities and their technological distance from the revolutionary core . This helps in understanding the knowledge base that underpins innovation in any one sector. In the modern competitive age firms continuously explore technological opportunities, improve their search procedures and refine their skills in developing and manufacturing new products. In particular market interactions select to different degrees and directions of technological development, allowing some firms to grow bigger and penalize others.

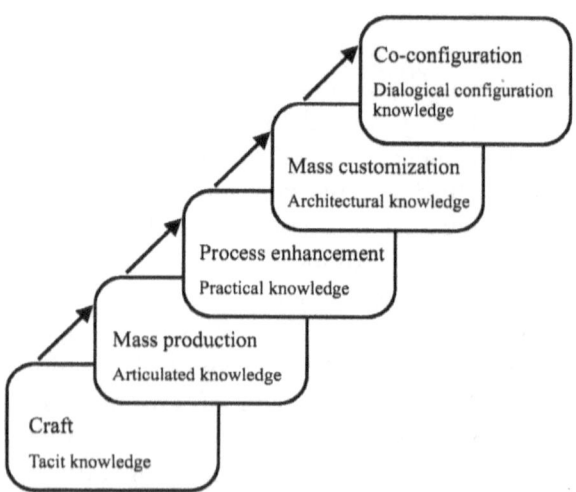

Sources: Victor and Boynton (1998); Engeström (2004); Virkkunen (2004)

Firm size and organization of research procure a full range of research services via the market, and if an in-house laboratory was critical to the utilization of research services that were available, research activity should have been incorporated within the firm above low levels of firm size. Firms that are first to commercialize a new product or process in the market. It is very important to commercialize the innovation which helps in providing a sustainable strategic advantage. The clear existence and persistence of this phenomenon may appear perplexing if not troubling. There should be a relationship between a variety of interfirm activities such as joint ventures, coproduction agreements, cross distribution arrangements and technology licensing. There is always a pre-paradigmatic design and the paradigmatic design phase can be calculated between the very two important functions process design and product design which restructures and maintains the most important part of innovation. There is always a core technology knowhow in innovation where the major functions like competitive manufacturing, distribution, service and complementary technologies are involved. As in different ways the Porters generic functions are determined, innovation too has many generic functions, where the broad factors depend upon specialized unilateral dependence of asset on the innovation, there is also a very important dependence and relations among each of these three functions from high effectivity to low effectiveness. The other factors are cospecialized bilateral dependence like container ships and ports and specialized unilateral dependence of innovation on the asset. To make a very specific analysis of the innovation gap and the ways that can determine it, it needs to analyze the investment required and the criticality of success. Both of these two factors are combined by a very important cost function and competitiveness or smartness to outsmart, which are both combined and added to the time function. It is very important to internalize the discrete activities and understand the major and minor possibilities and what is critical condition and non-critical condition. There are two important aspects that bring out the strategies and outcomes of a firm with legal and technical appropriability, they are as: Imitators and innovators advantageously positioned vis a vis independent owners of complementary assets, innovators and imitators disadvantageously positioned vis a vis independent owners of complementary assets.

In industries in which technological change of a particular kind has occurred which required deployment of specialized and or cospecialized assets at the time, a configuration of firm boundaries may well have arisen which no longer has compelling efficiencies. Existing firm boundaries may in some industries- especially where technological trajectory and attendant specialized asset matters draw a major distinction and outline.

There are very often particular possibilities that tend to be triggered by such circumstances as the following:

- A threat to current market share resulting from technological advances by a competitor yielding improvements in product capabilities or prices which are patently attracted to current or prospective customers.
- A progressively weakening competitive position which requires consideration of developing or adopting risky and costly new technologies as the most promising remaining means of safeguarding survival.
- A recent experience involving a technological innovation which yielded substantial competitive advantages as well as increased profitability and thus engender greater confidence in the practical potentials of additional such undertakings.
- Imminent commercial applicability of an internally developed technological innovation promising important market benefits.

There must be more emphasis to recognize and improve profitability and to concentrate more sharply on the specific product, process, costs and other adjustment targets involved in bettering past performance but there can be margins of error that can be involved in bettering past performance which can be more often done by using technical solutions through SAP and JD Edwards software or most efficiently solved by using the balanced scorecard. Redesigning of prototypes and benchmarking at the time of production brings a continuous reengineering process that helps in commercial use and new mark numbers.

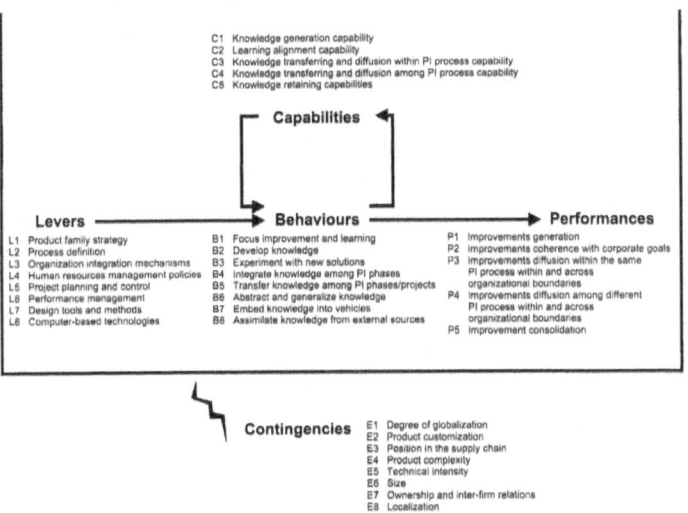

There is always a new product learning cycle that can be brought through lead customers and helps in developing customers through a large scale promotion that helps to measure an in depth understanding of the marketplace. It helps to develop a high contribution margin of the firm and helps to create a new technological skill of the business by understanding the market impacts. This brings a proper co-ordination of the firms business. It is important to make this function in places with a newness of market and a newness in technology. This helps to sharpen the focus of the existing organization and turn it into a self-empowered more stable reorganized organization. For using this idea the home base has to be made stronger.

It is very important to understand the supplier dominated firms, science-based firms, scale intensive firms and specialized equipment suppliers and draw a relationship between them to form the capacity and the inter-linkage and the impact and challenges they can produce. Firms that are sufficiently well linked helps in performing a very sophisticated innovation and invention plan that can help in understanding the criteria of development and be well versed with any type of business that is possible to perform with. In making a graphic analysis between software costs and the time involved in the business there should be use of specific applications program like CAD in any specialization or for personal use. Business graphics is also becoming an important phenomenon in todays world. There are many producers of comprehensive range of applications program and single applications program firms. All this is based on the source of innovations and the nature of business. Most of the innovation platforms are taken up by very large firms which use the highest computer control measurements in bringing effectiveness to its thinking.

The functional locus of innovation has many different predictions. Firstly the innovator has temporary monopoly power over the innovation information embodied in his output and capture significant benefit in embodying the knowledge in the output of his firm. Secondly the innovator has an imperfect ability to capture benefit from diffusing non-embodied information. Moreover licensing and diffusion of the innovation may be assumed freely to occur and derive the maximum value of benefit from the non-embodied knowledge capturable by the innovator via the patent mechanism which can be represented by licensing fees and other considerations received minus patenting and licensing costs incurred by the firm. There are many considerations like the impulse provided by the innovation that creates a potential for future adoption and there is a continuous retardation in the in the proportionate growth rate of adoption which approaches zero as diffusion approaches its equilibrium level. Improvements to general economic growth, changes in relative commodity and input prices and other complementary or competing innovations can be expected to occur during this process of diffusion.

There are many different ways by which there can be a product and process innovation. A very important development to look upon is performance-maximizing, sales maximizing, cost minimizing. All these important areas of development depend upon salesforce development and different competitive means that drive the value chain and Porters five forces. Cost is an important structure that can be reduced through vast study on process improvement, which brings about a change in performance which in turn affects the sales. If the firm does not look at the cost minimization factor then sales maximization does not turn up and the firm has to look at a very segmented or niche market outlook. In the process innovation the technology process is sometimes technology stimulated and cost stimulated with uncoordinated process leading to systemic process and product performance maximization leading to product cost minimization.

There are three basic roles of successful participants: firstly broad based competitors that can be reorganized to form and dominate in developing the highest level of strategy possible. Low cost producers which would be smaller firms with an emphasis on minimum costs and speciality firms that are small but geared at specific, high demanding semi-custom market niches. Thus it is systematic understanding of ideas that matter in diffusion and the economics of diffusion can be well arranged as in the points that has been discussed depending on the market situation and other preliminary strategy factors.

Chapter 3

(Baisham Chatterjee student UNBSJ)
Describing innovation and organizational impact

To look at the prospects of organizational impact, a firm should meet the demands that are easy to predict. First it is very important to look at the Canadian perspective. R&D is linked to new or significantly improve production or manufacturing processes. This seems to be a very broad sense of the organizational impact. Acquisition of machinery, equipment or technology is linked to very efficient manufacturing processes. Industrial engineering for start up is becoming a very significant area of improvement for Canadian firms. Tooling up and production start up is also very important for start and as a mini-US model these Canadian firm play a major challenge in boundaries, globalization and reaching across various countries unless acted upon by various HR power and innovation skills. It is also linked to identifying what the significant processes would be and it is very important to identify that at a later stage which Canadian firms have been able to and Canada has also been able to form innovative models through firms like Mariner Partners, J.D.Irving. Stantec probably leads in the sense of creativity in Canada and the firms that are more towards innovation are SMEs that get some help from NRC-IRAP and university research that lay the main foundation for their co-creation and innovativeness. JD Irving have better processes with lesser emphasis on increasing the number of branches, but more on situational strategy, employee ability and managing and making processes better. JD Irving gives more effort on product and brand effectiveness and improving the specialization and effectiveness of the products. JD Irving was one of the first Canadian firms that has kept on developing its model in innovation by using effectiveness through redesigning previous output measures and combining rapid innovation to sales. Production techniques are always looked to be one of the most suitable areas to learn and work upon. Similarly Mariner Partners created the first IPTV in Canada and has a great understanding and implementation of innovation, work ethics, and information and communications development. This two together brings the major challenge and focus in creating through collaboration as Mariner Partners has with Business bridges as well as integrating the leaders effort and the leadership and technocrats knowledge of Gerry Pond to the different technology creations and performance ability of Mariner Partners. There always needs to be a high cost of developing new or significant products or services. There is a necessity to develop projects or significantly improved products or services. There is often a lack of marketing capability to market significantly improved products due to a lack of information and communications, technical support and lack of expertise in universities. This can be reduced by creating the correct impact through understanding the challenge and analyzing the idea of reducing it. This seems to be a very big challenge and the main idea behind reducing this environment is co-creation, collaboration and understanding and measuring in tight situations.

All these operationalised factors can be developed by a variety of 4 forms of Network: variety of internal sources of information; variety of market sources of information; variety of research sources of information. Not very often but periodically it can be found that firms that count on a greater variety of internal sources of information were found to introduce world-first or Canada first informations. The policy implications deriving from these results are always very important, which are always very important. The step by step flowcharts and the contents in order of every process are very necessary to be derived and understood. These are generally the policies that follow a very prominent information, marketing, process implementation and utilization and environment step.

Information implication to understand patent counts is also very important. It involves counting the patents attributable to each firm within an industry and then performing tests to see whether higher patent counts correlate with higher firm performance. This can be implemented with the help of professional consultants deriving ideas through case study techniques and by research experts at research institutes located at particular cities and provinces and also by big research institutes like NRC-IRAP. The likelihood of performing R&D rises with firm size making it internally related within industries, it is also important to look at the rise of R&D to firm size thus helping develop on the implementation of new processes and developing internal consulting development between the firms growth and how the R&D should change with developing products.

Through all these forces coming into action, it is sometimes very difficult to deal with the demand function, where the environment is generally dominated by: threat from competitors, difficulty in hiring the right talent and retaining them through any mistake in HR or incentive, welfare policies. It is also very important to look at the rapid production and office technology changes. No product threats or difficulty in HR, creates a very serious error in the management board that can lead to a very serious mistake and abnormality in the forecasting or futuristic analysis.

The coefficients between the innovation indicators are recorded. Patents, trademarks and copyrights are highly correlated with both R&D and engineering and design. This is not surprising being given that R&D and industrial engineering and industrial design are innovation inputs for technology invention. Secondly acquisition of technologies is highly correlated with engineering and design, but less correlated with R&D. Engineering and design are two significant indicators for technology invention and R&D. Taking the implication of IPRs it can be noted that:

- Smaller firms are less likely than larger firms to use any or all IPR instruments. The relationship was statistically significant for use of all IPRs except trade secrets. This finding corroborates the hypothesis that for SMEs, cost considerations may discourage the use of IPRs other than trade secrets.
- Firms carrying out R&D and especially those doing so in a separate R&D unit or contracting out R&D, were also more likely than firms not involved in R&D to use any or all IPR instruments.
- Innovating firms, especially those that introduced world-first innovations to a lesser extent, firms that introduced Canada first innovations were likely to use IPRs.
- Firms that reported receiving a government subsidy for their R&D activity were more likely to use patents, trademarks and confidentiality agreements.

R&D is only one of the innovation inputs, and the cost of the R&D represents less than half of the total cost of innovation in Canada. Basic and applied research accounted for only 17% and development expenditures for 30% of total innovation cost. R&D expenditures in the European Commission has been termed to range from 25% of total innovation expenditures in electrical production to just 10% in the pulp and paper sector. It is a total of breakthroughs that helps in developing these R&D processes. Technology content tends to be a part of this and moreover IPRs and creative learning tends to be a part of the decisions taken by SMEs, their ability for technology sharing and their ability to build in or develop alliances with other organizational majors.

It is not only so that a firm has to take random decisions after an R&D decision is taken. Marketing is the compulsory idea behind removing prototypes. The major idea behind this is satisfying existing clients, developing new products and processes, promoting firm or product reputation, developing export markets and seeking new markets. There are many objectives of innovation which are as improving product quality, reducing environmental damage, dealing with better and more prominent and stable governmental regulation. As well as improve production flexibility. All these functions seem to depend more often on the paradigm shift and rules and regulations that mean for the welfare of the country. World trade and business reports as by Richard E Caves and data on organizational development strategies are the greatest impetus for a very farsighted growth. Moreover to understand the future prospects a firm should keep a balanced measurement between innovation and strategy implementation. There are many ways to acquire the knowledge that leads to innovation. Such knowledge need not be acquired exclusively through innovation activities carried out within a firm such as internal R&D. Technology can be acquired in the form of patents, non-patents inventions, licences, know-how, trademarks, services with a technological content. These services can be made mobile only if there is a proper coordination of all these through internal communication skills and proper understanding of these major challenges.

Contracted R&D is sometimes very important when the firm suffers from locational deficiencies, misallocation of resources and lack of proper suppliers. Porters five forces sometimes shows a negative in the economies of scale or not so well integrated technology, showing that contracted R&D

with already established brand names or universities are important at certain stages. It helps to perform R&D within the firm that is important to the firms success, helps in R&D staffs information, communication, practical knowledge and linkage development. Contracting R&D sometimes seems to be totally on the basis of the hierarchy who develop the needs of R&D and ways to make new decisions. If someone follows decision making then that seems to be the major focus and symptom of growth. R&D thus brings self-sufficiency to the development of a firm.

BUYER EXPERIENCE CYCLE - UNDERSTANDING BUYER IDEA

PURCHASE	PERFECTION	USE	BUYER VIEWS	SELF - SERVICE	DISPOSAL

COMPETITIVE MEASURES

ANALYZING SUPPLEMENTS	PRICES	PROMOTIONAL ARTICLES & MAGAZINES	OTHER BUYERS	SERVICE QUALITY	BRAND CHANGE

TRAINING , DEVELOPMENT (PRODUCT) IDEAS

TRAINING SERVICE PEOPLE	PERCEPTION OF PRODUCT	MARKET REACTION	SYSTEMATIC PRODUCT PERFORMANCE	PRODUCT SERVICE GUARANTEE	PROMOTIONAL & PROCESS PLANS

DEVELOPMENT OF INNOVATION TECHNIQUES

COST CUTTING	DUPLICITY REMOVAL	REDUCE INVENTORY	INCREASE HIGH FIDELITY EXPERIMENTS	RESOURCE UTILIZATION	INCREASED RESEARCH ON DESIGN AND ORGANIZATIONAL INNOVATION

B . CHATTERJEE (2009)

R&D is the basis for creating organizations for the future. But the implications to start with a better organizational future can be justified by saying that the future of organizations can be more broadly classified for firms that are a leading group of giant corporations branching out all over the world, with less global organizations marching up- hundreds of them with subsidiaries and associates in a multitude of countries and thousands of them at the building of the empire building activities. This is formed by organizational communication pattern, changes in knowledge, changes in technology etc. these are all a past data on preference. But to look at the present situation we also have to look at the cost reducing factors for organizational innovation. Its main ideas for reducing costs, saving time, rich in format, collaboration and integrated and distributed computing environment. Many of the intranet concerns are security, management commitment, reducing training hassle by state of the art system, in-house development and outsourcing and technologies selection.

To understand the innovation activity we should understand the intra project and the inter project dynamics of a firm. The companys processes via the internet from the patent stage to the first market tests is highly innovative. It is totally based on power point slides marketing via concept through conversation by use of internet communications. There is also necessity for influence of initial text and traces of strategic presentation in conversations. A phase of language study is dependant on organizational resources. A very ordinary research framework shows that 4 important dimensions of innovation are very strongly related and form a linkage with knowledge accumulation. Environment uncertainty, environment change frequency, environment complexity and environment change scale are parts of external environment and are always related to any form of knowledge type and its different sub components, culture and administrative and technical innovation. Organizational learning and market orientation are different forms of organizational learning. When something important happens to a major customer or market, the whole business unit is informed within a short period. Market responsiveness depends on competitors price and changes leading from its various product portfolio to business needs. In the revised learning process information acquisition, information distribution, information interpretation are interrelated to organizational memory. Information is a key source to bringing value and develop competitive intelligence.

There is also the topic of a very noted factor known as total management technique. There is no significant difference between TMT management styles, decision-making modes and there is always a significant difference in their study. Employee perceptions of support for innovation will be positively related to perceptions of management support, cohesion, organizational reward system and impartiality. Inability to overcome the nature and content of organizational innovation , can lead to workload pressures. Mechanism for continuous improvement addresses management of revision and improvement mechanisms for former projects and current projects that influence organizational innovation. Exploring internal knowledge generated is also very important. External knowledge acquisition and exchange addresses management of external information influencing organizational innovation in terms of competition, market, acquisition and the communication of technology. Decisions should be accepted with modification i.e change in sales to total sales ; change in profit due to product change to total profit and change in overall productivity due to product change. The number of patents obtained and R&D contribution, expenditure and commitment shows the true policy and ability that lies within organizational innovation. There are also necessity of contribution and idea generation on behalf of the R&D team or joint problem solving teams or matrix organizations, committees and task forces and project managers and formal meetings. Sometimes matrix organizations or any creative organizations has to operate at the lowest possible cost. Within this the 4 stages are preliminary concept development, design and development, validation of the idea or the product information starting from how to deal with the new product to building relationships with end customers. It is also very important to bring about an in service product support consisting of product review release, program completion and program review. Organizational innovation and organizational learning are the determining factors of entrepreneurship where personal mastery, transformational leadership, shared vision, proactivity and environment creates the major form of origination of organizational innovation and are the major focus areas to be learnt.

In a simple model for innovation it can be found that innovation culture is related to 4 different factors intention for innovation, infrastructure for innovation, market orientation for innovation and implementation context for innovation which all together leads to performance outcomes. There are few very critical constituents of innovation propensity and any other constituents for performance in innovation:

- Innovation propensity combines with innovation intention to develop within its business model and architecture to develop and sustain innovation which can be communicated through vision, goals, objectives. Innovation intention is also related to organizational constituency to develop innovation imperative and develop, value, equity, and contributions made within the organization.
- Similarly innovation infrastructure is related to organizational learning and creativity and empowerment to architect the greatest creativity in HR and self development.
- Similarly innovation influence is related to market orientation and value orientation by understanding the competitive forces as well as the clusters in which they operate.

Similarly organization innovation helps in understanding the motivation-threat –ability of a firm. Organizational complacency and switching costs are the key areas of motivation and are related to market orientation. Similarly technological uncertainty and political threats are a time when the firm looks at product championship. It is also the firms ability to specialize on these two things formalization structure and centralization structure which are affected by specialization and all these are together related or contributes to the organizational resistance to technological innovation.

Information technology, learning strategy, trust culture and flexible structure and design are the organizational contexts which are directly related to knowledge transfer that creates the main ideas on innovation talked about like innovation capabilities and organizational performance. Social performance, economic performance and comparative performance are the key areas that drives performance and are the key to organizational outlook and reorientation.

Technological change, organizational change and internal diffusion are closely linked to one another or rather they are integrated in the same system. Similarly they are related to people and organizational arrangements and stack resources. Other factors involved are output of the innovation process and organization of the innovation process which consists of goals pursued consisting of goals achieved which comprises of state of the operating core prior to the adoption of FMS, adaptations made. Other important part is goals not partially achieved consisting of technical problems, organizational bottlenecks and market changes. Sometimes very often goals are always achieved. This is when new system is perceived as better than the prior system because of: Web-enablement; ability to integrate with ERP and multiple supply chain functions. Organizational knowledge creation consists of both individual and inter-organization which is generally bounded in the area between explicit knowledge and tacit knowledge bounded by externalization and internalization of the knowledge. It is generally termed that knowledge that can be well integrated, interpreted and institutionalized are sociable and a combination on all this develops the skills for organizational learning.

Customers needs, the number and types of competitors, and the range of all technological possibilities are all characterized by frequent and substantial change. Given this dynamic environment, minimizing time to market has become a high priority for a broad range of firms. It creates new organizational capabilities and innovative ways to use resources. Firms unable to maintain price or cost advantages will need to shift to a knowledge focus and rapid development and adoption of new technologies, systems and processes. Below is a diagram that shows the linkage between leverages, behaviors and performances and the capabilities that manipulates it. This is also well connected by certain contingency factors.

For developing an organizational perspective. It is very important to understand and develop vision and objectives, understand existing processes, identify process for redesign, identify change levers, implement the new process, make new process operational, evaluate the new process and make ongoing continuous improvement. This is a key idea behind process improvement and its follow up for product innovation.

Technology related innovativeness represents a basic willingness to depart from existing technologies or practices and venture beyond the current state of art. It helps in developing new environmental opportunities and indicates behavioral change and may refer to the degree to which an individual or other unit of adoption is relatively earlier in adopting new ideas than any other member of the system. Innovativeness is considered to be either the ability of generating new ideas or combine new sources for receptivity to new ideas. Acknowledgements of the danger of organizational ineffectiveness in the case of radical implementation and use of the new processes. The criteria behind this is improved information sharing and assessment of the impact of the limitations of the existing processes on organizational effectiveness. Customer orientation in the case of CI or continuous improvement in processes of organizational learning defines quality as internal as well as external, breaking processes into basic tasks and improvement of both products and processes. CI also helps in defining new techniques thus making competition better and more easily understandable. Based on the CIMA model based on continuous innovation, behaviors underpinning CI and learning within product innovation, company contingencies, continuous learning.

Thus organizational innovation leads to improvement of internal as well as external processes which justifies that processes are created by goals and all these ideas behind reaching these goals.

Chapter 4

(Baisham Chatterjee student UNBSJ) Developing on the locational theory and performance management

The locational theory is based on years of expertise and work on developing very indispensible manufacturing firms. The Webers theory is based upon three general factors of location and the most important to start with. Innovation carries a major dependence on location of a firm from which economies of scope and scale come into action. The three factors are as : transportation costs, labor costs, and agglomerating forces. Although transportation is also becoming an international factor, inbound logistics is sometimes local when there are too many firm willing to be fed with resources, whereas these firms that export firms outside their country tend to derive very much of a global outlook . Hence making transportation costs both inbound and outbound a very important factor to think upon and setting the idea of least cost location. If cost of transfer is the only significant factor the site with the lowest transportation cost would be selected. As transportation costs, labor costs too cannot be ignored and both stand as an the premier focus in manufacturing.

Another important area of study is the Hoovers cost factors of location: the transportation factors and production factors. Cost of procuring the raw materials and cost of distributing the finished products are considered as transport costs. The studies which attempt explanation of the size and shape of the firm's market area are closely related to others that stress the locational interdependence of the firm. The hypothesis of locations shows two types of locations either movable locations (without costs) or planned future locations. Markets are identified in various ways like: cost of production are equal at all locations, but the freight rate of final good is higher in one zone than the other. Transporting the final good is not too significant a part of delivered to customer costs. The spatial interdependence of locations depends on: spatial scattering of consumers, infinitely elastic demand for the product of an industry, equal costs of procuring and processing raw materials at all locations.

A higher concentration of the industry takes place when marginal costs, at points distant from the origin are increasing more than freight costs to take place. In this case dispersion of firms is promoted by a willingness of each firm to compete actively in price. If a firm does not compete in price and rather adopts as its net-mill price the base mill price of the price leader, plus its freight cost, the distant location will be most profitable, only if its price is greater than that of the price leader by at least an amount equally and invertedly proportional to the smaller number of sales it obtains at a distant location as compared to the sales that would be gained at the location of the price leader. Apart from unequal costs at alternative locations and uneven scatter of populations, the existence of price leadership that encourages industrial concentration. When firms neither compete actively in price nor follow the price of rivals, but rather seek to supply proportionate shares over parts of the market, the equilibrium price which results when a new rival enters and locates at a distance is lower than that price which results if he located next to the existing rival. Monopoloid leadership or proportionate share of supply over market segments: gains advantage in costs, expects to obtain custom by locating near selected consumers and competition in space may cause higher manufacturing prices than that which would exist in the absence of such competition.

Where firms do not open symmetrically, they are by the very nature of the case sufficiently close together so that the attempt by way of site selection and associate price policy to dominate some part of the market area otherwise belonging to another provides competitive policy in regard to location and price. Assessing the cost factor is also a very important skill, but its availability thereof is a cost reducing factor; the unit price of advertising is a cost factor; but the decrease in advertising units needed because of special protection is a cost reducing factor. All least-cost locations tributary to all consuming centers, are equal in cost and thus the plant locator selects the least-cost location which is tributary to the consuming centers that offers the greatest sales potential. In many a case the subject firm conceived of demand forces other than movement nearer to or further away from competitors. The cost factors of location in some cases makes the demand factor significant because the revenue increasing forces were so pronounced in this case makes or establishes in each business establishment to monopolize a particular segment of the market through lower delivered prices. The locational competitiveness of an industry is another consideration in the location of the demand influence.

Another important locational factor theory is the Thunen-Weber type of theory which emphasizes:

- Emphasis on the search for the site offering least cost, which provides the unique substitution among different factor costs that yields the optimum cost position.
- There should always be a locational selection that defines the interdependence of firms with three main aspects, like site selection which involves substitution among not only the cost factors at alternative locations but also the demand factors at different sites.

- Market demand is a factor that is derived from modern linkage and firms overcome trouble through this linkage and thus the market demand and power to support this demand increases automatically.

Few factors that measures unequal costs are adoption of prices that determines the uncertainty of the situation. To avoid this the firm has to look at the periodical objective that would ascertain the plant location:

- Firms seek for a least-cost location and understand the force of concentration that is greater in the event of unequal costs at alternative locations than in the case of equal costs at all sites, it all depends on the elasticity of the demand function and characteristic of marginal cost. In some cases the location management is the basis and capstone in increasing performance management.

These are all a very staunch feature to locate as to where the firm performance should go. A company must also know the costs of its entire economic chain. It must work with all the other businesses that contribute to the final product which would share compatible information sharing across companies. Price-led costing in which the customer is willing to pay determines allowable costs, will start the potentiality of economic chain costing. There are different informations like foundation, productivity information etc. There are many indicators of business performance which are a key critical factor of innovation. Its different parts are quality, customer satisfaction, innovation , market share. Information architecture is very important for this. Diversity in products, markets, and business units puts a big strain on rules and theories developed for smaller, less complex organizations. Very often successful performance in global markets is not possible and investments are very difficult to sustain because of the complex performance matters created as in the last sentence. In contrast internal yardsticks that measure current performance in relation to prior period results, current budgets or the results of other units within the company have an important visual understanding. Thanks to dramatically improved price-performance ratios in hardware and to breakthroughs in software and database technology, organizations are able to store more information. Firms that specialize in strategy formulation, often have well developed methods for assessing market share and other performance metrics. Similarly non-value added activities contribute to its current cost. Similarly if a given distribution channel or market is unprofitable the company can reduce costs in various ways to make it profitable. Cost reduction may be activity, volume maximization, software implementation, vendors etc. If the company lowers the price of a product to reduce sales volume, then the impact for cost per unit has to be decided. Where the design and engineering stages of a product has to be avoided, unnecessary circumstances has to be overcome.

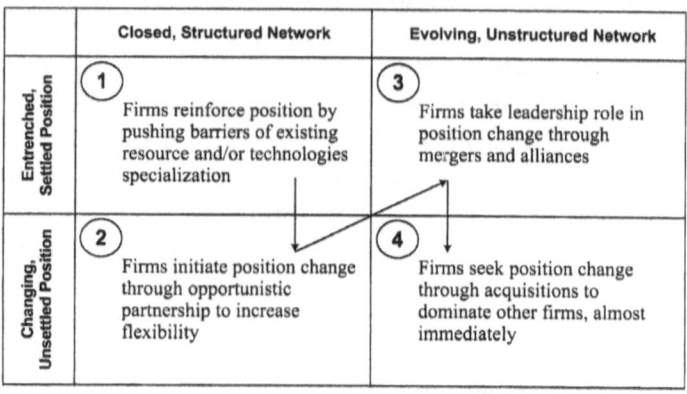

Similarly there are classic business ratios for measuring performance- all the three important areas of interest- return of equity, return on assets and return on sales. ROM or return on management is a very new implication to understand this which stands as: productive organizational energy released divided by management time and attention invested. High ROM managers are explicit for example, in telling their employees what types of customers the organization will not accept, what types of products or initiatives it will not fund and what type of deals people should not do. In this case the strategic base for business opportunities has to be generated. Financial opportunities cannot generate more than $ 5 million in annual revenue. The competitive and product factors are also very critical,with the competition giving the firm an opportunity in the market. Products that cannot be mass produced can obtain a distinctive market position being for an only cause and its facilities, functions and features being unnecessary and useless to change. Sustainable technology can create such products, because as technology is getting more difficult to catch up with and is fast changing a low cost disruptive item that has better and more specific effect is more suitable to win. In the return on management too often employees succumb to the political hastles and the way the hierarchy can change policies or deal with its employees- such as information processing, employee satisfaction and revenue growth. Managers and employees are very often accountable for performance and they select different diagnostic measures to focus on product development and customer service.

Many managers fail to realize the traditional measures, which focus on results, may help them keep score on the performance of their businesses, but do not help a multifunctional team monitor the activities or capabilities that enable it to perform a given process. Performance measurement systems should reflect operating assumptions which should be made control based.

Contracts very often define the product and helps in creating a targeted cost through the help of basic financial information like: cost of goods sold (including cost of revenues+ benefits through past performance+ analyzing benefits in present performance), gross margins, revenues. During the entire design phase people think of certain features like performance costs, analyzing the important prototypes and using cost functions to remove these prototypes and bring originality. Other costs involved are development costs and the maintenance costs (costs involved in maintaining the hierarchy that helps in understanding the training and its utilization of quality engineers, plants quality and ways on improving on it, as well as understanding product and resource boundaries). If the product scenario and the measures to constantly recreate it through understanding the environment in well understood, then the firm looks at process measures: like defining the types of factors like time, cost, quality and mapping the cross-functional process that help in delivering results and identifying the critical terms and capabilities that help in measuring the other relative terms.. With all this information the product development project ends with figuring out how to reduce cycle time without sacrificing quality.

Balanced scorecard for performance management is the most important factor and the most considerable area of work to deal with for performance enhancement in any field , whether it may be innovation or software implementation or employee relationship. Kaplan and Norton came up with the idea to develop an the prospect of businesses and changing the prospect of modern business thinking:

- As we depend on the connectivity between marketing, finance and HR in the fundamentals of management, similarly we think of few very important aspects to discuss with and connecting them in the balanced business scorecard perspective. It is very important to measure the quarterly growth,ROI and the different yearly or monthly financial returns including equity to improve on.
- Customer perspective is also very important relating to new products, responsive supply, preferred supply

and customer partnership. It gives a more diverse and broad focus on CRM including the channels that would measure the retention of new products.
- Internal business perspective and innovation and learning perspective develops the excellence based on technological capability and measuring the relationship between new product introduction and time to market.

There is a necessity for using the quality and cycle-time improvement programs where the newly created capacity can be created. To capitalize on this self-created new capacity companies must expand sales to completely new customers because of the improved quality and delivery performance. In calculating cycle time measurements three divisional examples are achieved. For example there is no premium earned for early delivery and the contracts allow for reimbursements of inventory holding costs. Hence there are no benefits when the customer is willing to pay. The only benefits from reduction in cycle time or industry reduction occur when reduction in factory floor complexity leads to real reduction in product costs. This process of building a machinery in the current build cycle in order to forecast leads to high inventory-more than twice the levels of our other businesses and overstocking and obsolescence of equipment. If build cycle time could be reduced less than the six-week ordering time then a breakthrough occurs. The breakthrough makes things very predictable and promising by shifting to a build-to-order schedule and eliminate the excess inventory occurring from building to forecasts. There should be cycle time reductions when the cycle time drops below a critical level.

Quarterly statistics as stated before helps in achieving progress in long-term objectives and achieve progress in understanding the proper balance between short-term and long-term performance. It is very important to understand control and and short term focus to understand breakthrough performance.

There are many unique strategies for developing and controlling techniques. In order it is followed as: translating the vision- building a consensus around the company's strategy. The second being communicating and linking, the second being business planning and the third feedback and learning. There are always four very important perspectives for developing on company growth as usual: but the most important of them being internal business process:which means reworking the strategies, and learning and growth :which consists of employee morale and employee suggestions. If all these are combined together, it gives a much definite and unique result in few cases.

If all these ideas goes very far then it helps in clarifying and translating the vision and strategy, communicating and linking, strategic feedback and learning and planning and target setting. All these combine together to give the most preferable outlook in balanced scorecard that can be undertaken by the senior hierarchy or innovator.

Chapter 5

(Baisham Chatterjee student UNBSJ)
Integrated companies: how they work

Integrated companies are formed not only with the means of, or for the cause of integrating different departments including the marketing and communications. But today integrated product design is the key factor where it is intended to form a design entity that satisfies marketing, functional, technical, manufacturing and aesthetic requirements. It is to achieve the highest customer satisfaction with lowest possible cost. A method for assembly design evaluation and a criteria for redesign is also established. There are certain guidelines in the redesign phase that are always important, the design process should result in a product with low assembly cost.

In the modern sense of concentrating on the product design, a company can adopt the strategy of minimum cost. For product design, modularity which satisfies product variant requirements will lower the average unit cost of the product family. For production system it can adopt a strategy of using automated equipment and new production techniques to shorten the production time, reduce the cost, improve the reliability and increase the flexibility in handling product variances and small batches. IPD approach is a development mainly in small and medium-sized companies. There is a reverse process in the flowchart which starts with conceptual design that not only ascertains the production and cost control measures to understand the location and site for the manufacturability analysis. Moreover other things involved are part design for assembly which consists of understanding the different components, reengineering on them, look at the different processes of getting things together and also look towards retrofitting. Making a design analysis of the assembly system, both the process, prospects, components, supply chain and manufacturing process gap. After that comes the economic justification of recommending the system.

A few important point to depend upon after the economic justification is done is serialization of the design process where fewer people are required to carry out the integrated product design process. As in traditional system design the focus is mainly on local issues as global issues can be fixed by the channels or vendors who are willing to collaborate. The local issues are primarily technical such as parts feeding, assembly sequence problems, task assignments and system layout. Conceptual designs are proposed according to PDS or product design specification where the main measures are product structure, geometric features of components, joining techniques and assembly systems are prepared in advance. Through this phase products may be assembled by a flexible automatic system, only two assembly directions and three types of finger are important. Through this specification only one assembly direction is required, the number of components is reduced and components can be easily fed and grasped.

The above said factor is the first stage that brings us to the strategic process in integrated manufacturing. It is very necessary to develop on a strategic integration system. It helps in linking manufacturing practices to business needs and describes some of the tools which are being developed to operationalize the framework. External integration is the matching of the manufacturing objectives and policies to the needs of the market and the competitive needs of the company, looking at the environmental perspective. Firms should look at cost reduction which being the first priority of competitive strategy where the firm with the use of rapid communication systems, internet hot spots can help in communicating with firms by looking first at a local perspective. Looking at storing and deriving information as and when required creates a rapid response mechanism. These factors create the major factors in developing the policy area with facility, capacity, span of process, control policies, which all help in developing and retaining new products that create performance measures.

Customer feedback system (CFS) that facilitates learning and supports a customer driven orientation. It is the basis on which CRM is developed and consists of: service indicators, standards and performance targets; feedback collection tools and feedback process management; a reporting system; a service recovery system; an IT system; a team learning system and an organizational positioning of a CFS. In the CFS a relationship is created between the indicators, standards and targets. Where there is a very profound linkage between the service quality attributes consisting of physical interface, responsiveness, competence, internal and external communication management and credibility. The next stage is led by the processing time and then it comes to defining service quality goals for staff and the last one is defining process/ departmental service quality goals which is led by satisfying 80% of the applications within 3 days. There are two cases of centralized data and decentralized data in the feedback entry classification.

A particular aspect that can be dealt with in detail is the integration of the logistics part of the value chain via information flow. The few ideas that can also be given a major focus are also a major area of challenge in marketing and are as: time, place, form and customization where product life cycles are shortening because of the growing variability of demand, production and product technology and the competitors actions. All these being interrelated. Similarly a broader focus can be given by bringing in what has been left out. Like the application of postponed engineering, postponed purchasing, postponed components/ semi-finished product manufacturing, postponed packaging and labeling and postponed international distribution. It is said that ICT can somewhat reduce the innovation gap by reducing the gap between production, marketing and logistics that can be through SCM or locational and transport technology and time management software. This helps bringing close the knowledge intensive ideas in manufacturing. It is true that integrated technology and use of ICT to reduce the innovation gap is highly knowledge intensive.

Another part of a successful integrated technology is an FMS or flexible manufacturing system. Their major benefits are that they improve market performance, reduce cost of operations, improve operations management, look at spin-off and designing. There are many important functions for this, which consists of:

- Market advantages consisting of ease of product replacement, ease of product modification, improved product quality, shorter delivery date and reduced sales price.
- Operational advantages makes a very sharp contrast to the resources of the Porters five forces and consists of unmanned manufacturing, higher machine utilization, higher output rate, shorter processing times, smaller batch sizes and reduced scrap and rework.
- Spin-off on the other hand leads to standardization of design tools fixtures, application of latest technology, step towards further automation, new product launch and technical obsolescence of existing machines.
- These all together lead to direct labor, mechanization of operations and reduced costs by improving capacity.

Moreover to bring everything together it is very necessary to talk of TRM (or Total relationship management) on which very few assumptions have been made although it has been assumed that it has been formed to bring in the idea of long run profitability. It consists firstly of creating and managing a systematic market audit system that includes microenvironment forces and helps in developing competitive analysis. It also helps in creating and managing internal marketing, networks and planning. Thirdly it is important to manage relationship with subcontractors or suppliers who provide material or sub-component and contribute to organization improvement. Fourthly it is important to create and manage relationships with external collaborators who contribute to the organizations improvement, success and long term growth. The fifth point relates to creating and managing relationships with distributors and it is important to create and care for professional relationship with them. At last it can be said that it is important to create and manage mutual profitable and fair relationships with customers.

Business transformation process	X → ☐ → Y		
Goal	Reach the critical mass by building an installed base of customer	Improve transformation process efficiency	Create numerous innovative information services
Strategy	<ul><li>Achieve demand-side economies of scale</li><li>Increase installed customer base's collective switching costs</li><li>Reduce customer's transaction costs (i.e., make it easy for customers to do business with you)</li></ul>	<ul><li>Apply conventional management techniques (e.g., TQM, process re-engineering) to improve efficiency</li><li>Achieve supply-side economies of scale and scope to reduce supply-side switching costs (R&D and setup costs)</li><li>Lower transaction costs in the digital economy enables companies to design new organizational structures and to reconfigure value creation systems for enhanced value creation</li></ul>	<ul><li>Transform value proposition by taking advantage of the demand-side economies of scope</li><li>Increase user's (or buyer's) switching costs by offering value across many different and disparate markets</li></ul>

There is also an integrated framework of key account management which is also to be studied in detail. KAM creates trials and errors and no opportunity for corporate learning. It is very necessary to understand the success factors and linkages of KAM programs. It is very important to structure the linkage and it consists of genesis, professionalization, internationalization and specialization. There are various relationships, components that are a key strategic issue of KAM. It grows with implementation and knowledge. The first being implementation and realization, the second being key supplier, the third being international and global KAM, job-profiles and tasks as well as professionalization of national KAM programs. But it is very necessary to find a solution to KAM. It is very important to find the willingness of the entire company to fulfill special needs of key accounts by itself or by business partners. It is very necessary to analyze KAMs influence on product service range. After this process of aligning comes the process of integrating where the innovative products and services were developed for key accounts into its general product and service and initiating it on basis of key accounts.

These above mentioned factors are all obscure factors. But to begin with the actual thing performance should be increased to improve the innovation management:

- The first generation corresponds to technology push. This era of innovation was the foundation for the industrial revolution. It came with the new technology advanced products and means of production. Such products are pushed onto the market.
- The second generation is a need pull concentrated with a shift to a market/customer focus and responding to product technology needs. The third generation is the coupling model which is involved with an era of push and pull models. The market might need new ideas, but production technology refined them.

R&D developed new ideas that marketing refined with market feedback.
- The fourth generation of innovation has an integrated model with a tight coupling of marketing and R&D activity together with strong supplier linkages. The fifth generation consists of the systems integration and networking model and are all strongly linked to collaborative marketing.
- It is very true that in the modern era of innovation the different sources of innovation are as: the introduction of new products or services, continuous improvement on work processes, radical change through increasing focus on BPR and marketing and sales, improving staff competence and using efforts to improve supplier performance.

To look towards the innovation management perspective directly from the point of view of the society or making the modern perspective of innovation look brighter. It can be addressed that globalization is important in this period of innovation at a time when international competition increases and organizations realize the strategic importance of technologies. There is also a lot of innovation in alliances with parallel and integrated innovation, from innovation to the business development (NBD). Innovation management means managing research links and external research environments. Parallel processes are used to involve multiple actors and to increase the development speed. The 4th generation includes business and market models in innovation with coordinated process of innovation among a network of partners. The required coordination is often attained by system integration with key suppliers and customers and parallel development of components or modules of innovation.

Communications does not seem so complicated to deal with. What is more important is dealing with CIM or computer integrated manufacturing system. CIM needs strategic justification, cost justification and benefit needs. Strategic justification is involved with market assessments i.e. where customers want the improvements offered by CIM i.e, better quality and improved delivery times. Assess how competitors are currently positioned in terms of the improvements CIM would offer. Other important areas to work on would be determining areas of opportunity and forecasting the shifts of technology and its impacts. Radical improvement, business process reengineering, and incremental improvement are the other areas to work on giving a strong HR focus as well as value innovation focus.

Chapter 6

(Baisham Chatterjee student UNBSJ). Management techniques for managing innovation

The technical process of innovation carries a lot of aspects from bringing new products and processes into the market place- consists of many small steps from thinking to selling it. Moreover all technical innovations may be different at the end or when the project is in continuation but the theoretical aspects is all the same. It is management measurement that counts the most in all decisions relating to innovation or understanding where and when the project should end. There are generally 3 phases where the first phase consists of establishing climate of innovation, constructing innovation investment portfolio, developing organizational structure to support innovation and defining product and process goals. The second phase consists of research and development which consists of information search, basic research and preliminary planning. Other factors are testing the patent plans and understanding and making a basic note of designing, engineering and testing the product on which changes and diversifications are going to be made. This requires a very deep concentration on R&D. It is also very important to develop preliminary market plans. The third phase consists of diffusion which can also be termed as getting all the right ideas together. It consists of developing formal market plans, establishing market introductions and responding to market needs. There are various processes involved like innovation incentives , innovation training , quality circles which all combine to make a product or innovation idea perfect. There are many technical barriers involved in innovation which are like lack of technical information, lack of support for collateral invention and lack of other technical resources. It is important to plan innovation in a structured process. The structured process helps in nurturing innovative ideas through group dynamics. It is very important to provide intensive capital and initiate mature firm's development and growth. It is very important to provide financial support to industries with high R&D costs, ensuring technological advancement and reduction of risk borne to technology developers. There are also many licensing factors that are involved in encouraging the transfer of new product/process ideas among licensee network participants. This is an advantage for lack of support for collateral invention. They centralize technical resources required to stimulate the planning of innovation.

In the industrial applications centre there are innumerable technical barriers involved which has a lot of technical information filtration involved in it. In this case barriers are high because it disseminates new product and process concepts to industry. The lack of support for collateral invention matches technological resources with industrial needs to define new applications for products and services. The lack of other technical barriers is high and provides previously developed technology to affect newly defined market needs. Although the barriers for helping entrepreneurs depend upon low-risk supportive environment and helping in developing innovative ideas. Another important factor involved is technology transfer from laboratories where the main thrust is on developing connectivity and relationship in understanding the relationship between R&D /marketing, participants, new technology which would help to understand concepts to develop innovation creation ideas. Understanding the problems, risks and assigning the right work to the employees as well as developing communications perspective to understand the channels and industry-university relationships that would help in understanding the marketing and the different probabilities involved.

The Delphi technique first developed by RAND Corporation is a very important and basic technique to start with. Here the group of creative innovators is given a single problem on which to focus. The major challenge of the group is to provide with numerous ideas for the most possible solutions of the problem. The focus group and the key brainstorming session are involved in this.

The compensation plan plays a major role as innovation incentive and is probably a very important and sustainable challenge to create organizational incentive. It is very important to identify professional staff to be affected by compensation plan. The R&D staff in different groups of the firms business makes a comparative understanding to understand the compensation required to understand the primary and major challenges in the firms business. Forecasting helps to relocate the priority of a firms business and with time there needs to be a continuous reconstruction of the salary grades, professional and performance benefits and reviewing the objectives periodically.

Organizational development is a very important set of developmental ideas that help in different transformations. It is a collection of certain set of ideas like sensitivity training, group-problem solving or team building that helps in providing a secure path between organizational goals and its employees who give the right effort. There is a close relationship between the management system maintained by an organization and performance or results. Beginnings is sometimes very critical where the structure of management style seems very difficult. But a proper idea on modern technology research, new and emerging technologies as well as performance management applied both in the technology advancement and step by step product reengineering or management planning is important to develop idea on developing the foremost challenge base for the company or the product. Majority of the American businesses or German businesses are based on related products or related businesses where major challenges and value implementation played in one segment helps in bringing out a sustainable development in other segments by understanding its core competence. Similar is the case with chemical firms, automotive firms or heavy engineering firms. Firms with a high level of competence in technology development prove to operate and known to be high performers in all its related segments. Similarly Canadian research organizations like NRC-IRAP has a high sense of credibility in developing high performing mid-sized businesses in Canada. Most of the Canadian firms are a replica of American businesses but the major credibility of Canadian firms don't usually go to developing ideas through their self created research centres but from patent rights or ideas from NRC-IRAP or research centres like MITRE Corporation which both together develop the highest involvement with industries in research, and protection of patent rights and investment in new businesses. Similarly the Wallace McCain Institute in New Brunswick helps in combining technology with entrepreneurial talent to develop future leaders.

New product development projects managed by new venture groups commonly pass through four distinct phases from generation to commercialization. During the first phase the technical and commercial evaluations of the new product or process concept are conducted. Often this first phase of new product development is performed by the innovator and management within the traditional organizational framework. During the second phase the new venture team is formalized and a detailed plan of development is constructed. In this situation of developing the business plan product profitability is analyzed. Marketing and market analysis tends to be a major rule of the game and the third phase of the project is characterized by major product and market development activities. During the last and fourth phase the new product is marketed through a new and existing corporate divison, or is licensed and spun off into a free-standing enterprise.

There is always a survey sample of staff involved in technical projects and there is a necessity to identify dimensions of project performance which affect project success. They also characterize determinants of successful project dimensions. There needs to be a pretest list of project dimensions and determinants and prepare project description questionnaire. Another important factor that counts in the end at the time of filtration of all the ideas is strong and weak points of project management and operation and at the end is a review and analysis which suggests the most important areas of progress and how next generation projects can be rectified and made better. Projects take time to find a path or take a right direction and in bringing huge construction projects to completion it is very important to think of the three foremost things: management structure, patience and managing the most important hurdles of time. All these factors are related to the important circumstances that lead to managing the environment , like disaster management, uncertainty management, resource calculation, usage and utilization and logistics. At present few areas like supply chain focus and its key specifications like purchasing or building a management and technology framework or a strategic plan before building and constructing the bridge or the dam which all falls under the major chunk of enterprise resource planning. As projects are becoming bigger and more difficult to manage it is very important to focus more on enterprise resource management rather than operations and implement SAP ERP or J.D.Edwards for faster process, correct calculations and quicker results.

There are many management techniques involved in one or more new product development projects. It is based on the major determinants of the project performance. The major determinants are manufacturing and business performance which is based on financial returns. Other things involved are technical performance and efficiency, personal growth experience and technological innovativeness. The external environment depends on management support, interorganizational relations, sponsor relations, transfer management which is based on timeliness, planning, priority assignment. A very important role is played by the project leader who creates the foremost importance towards coordination of decisions. Quality circles help in developing new products and processes in manufacturing. Corporate guidelines need to be developed for the establishment of quality circles, the second step involves to educate potential participants of quality circles. Formalization of the quality circle ideas and revise technical support are other important areas to plan, confirm, execute and improve on.

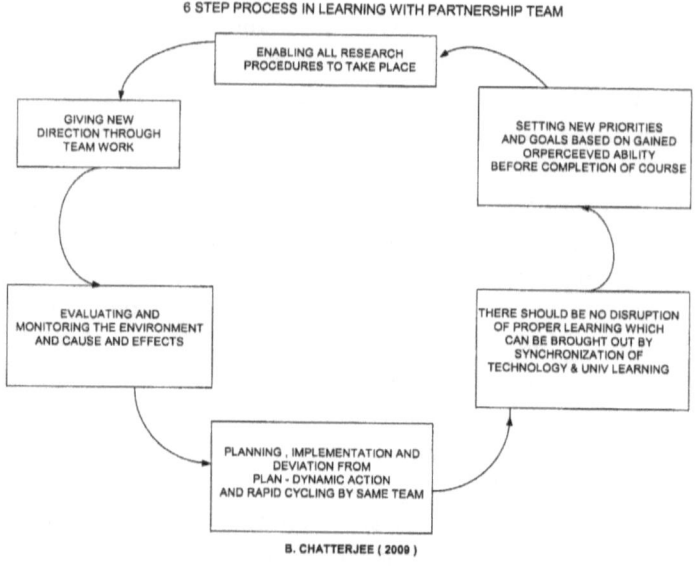

There are important research planning frames that can be prepared in different situations depending on the corporate concept: there are different corporate concepts developed based on the size of the firm, the business linkage and the expansion plans and path goal theory. Which helps in determining feasibility of complicated projects, review technology and prepare recommendations for new products & processes. Sometimes temporary groups help in corporate feasibility but for projects that take a long time to be completed or have barriers in each step need to reconstruct with a permanent very highly sophisticated technical group. This kind of technology arises in highly sophisticated large quantity contract based instrument manufacturing, designing plans for new technology businesses or power projects and nuclear projects. In this case a group with compensation incentives based on retirement time as well as time based and performance based incentives help in activating the process with more effectiveness.

There are also many relevant areas towards licensing of a product like:

- when a new product has been developed by a firm with limited marketing capabilities, the value of the technology can be increased if licenses to manufacture and sell the product are granted to other firms.
- When the product does not lie within the companys principal business, a spin-off technology can be more easily marketed by a firm in the relevant industry
- When the company that has developed the new product does not have the financial resources, it cannot support adequate commercial development of the new product.
- Cross-license helps in trading rights when two company's want each other's proprietary technology.
- In the case of manufacturing an item important to its own needs, but cannot be bothered with the actual manufacture.

Other R&D efforts that should be utilized are maximizing the relationship between industry-university partnerships that helps in conceptualizing the requirements and necessities of funds and understanding the sponsors and its relationship with technical work areas. The utilization of resources and mutual understanding between these two different areas should be understood for allocating resources and authority to the different research units of the organization.

BUSINESS STRATEGY THAT BRINGS UNIV COMPANY CLOSER

```
┌─────────────────┐      ┌──────────────────────────────────────────┐
│ VISION          │ ───► │ BUSINESS AND FUTURE STRATEGY OUT LOOK    │ ──►
│ CREATIVITY      │ ───► │  • CORE PRODUCTS OF COMPANY - UNIV       │
│ TARGETS         │ ───► │  • CORE MARKETS THE UNIV                 │
│ GOALS           │ ───► │  • CORE CUSTOMERS DIFFERENT COUNTRIES    │
│                 │      │    COMPETITIVE ADVANTAGES                │
│                 │      │    TO MAKE BETTER AND DEVELOPING         │
│                 │      │    RELATIONSHIP                          │
└─────────────────┘      └──────────────────────────────────────────┘

     ┌──────────────────────────────────────────────────────────────┐
  ◄──│ KEY TASKS        ──►  ORGANIZATION CORE EMPLOYEES            │
     │ KEY COMPETENCES  ──►  UNDERSTAND CORE COMPETENCES IN         │
     │                       DIFFERENT SUBJECTS THAT HELP IN        │
     │                       THE LEARNING PROCESS.                  │
     │                                                              │
     │                    •  DEVELOPMENTAL AND INFRASTRUCTURE       │
     │                       CHANGE PLAN                            │
     │                                                              │
     │ INVESTMENTS      ──►  BUDGETS                                │
     │ MARKETING        ──►  MARKETING PLANS                        │
     │ TIMING           ──►  MILE STONE                             │
     │ DEVELOPMENT      ──►  UNDERSTAND THE UNIVERSITY HISTORY      │
     │                       FOR FURTHER DEVELOPMENT                │
     └──────────────────────────────────────────────────────────────┘
```

B. CHATTERJEE (2009)

Some of the factors influencing the development of new products and processes outside large industry are increasing costs and market complexity. Costs for evaluation, business analysis, development and market analysis are very high. There is requirement of individual corporate and market feasibility, such as manufacturing facilities, existing product lines, well-defined markets and financial return requirements. Feasibility is a very important area to work on and it can be justified more through education, university research experience and hands on experience in large –scale R&D.

R&D funded by the federal government should demonstrate a definable link to a measurable health system goal. Medical technology contributions in health care industry does not lend itself to cost benefit analysis. High cost medical technology and medical diagnostic tools gives the greatest cost benefits. Medical specialists who use a high level of specialization technology are rewarded by the reimbursement system. This would lessen the pressure to continually develop new medical specialty equipment and services. Incentives to stimulate innovation outside the regulatory process are subsidies, procurement protocols established by the government, patents and structured information transfer.

NRC-IRAP is evaluated to have all these necessities and authorities to drive Canada forward. NRC helps in diagnosing emerging opportunities, proactively facilitate growth of cluster infrastructure and accelerating the flow of knowledge and technology to groups of firms. It helps in forging connections within cluster supply chains regionally nationally and internationally. NRC provides an important standing in measuring projects through market intelligence, linking firms through clusters and collaboration and understanding and analyzing self productivity. Often it is difficult to understand productive output but building technology clusters and an ability to manage and sustain them have been the greatest output and perfectionism of NRC. Sometimes it seems difficult of how this can be managed by such a big research infrastructure organization. This is when investments and deep understanding of competitive strategy comes into play by combining technology with competitive strategy.

Chapter 7

(Baisham Chatterjee student UNBSJ) Different factors to find the innovation gap and improve on it

Its all competition that is given a genuine focus before finding the innovation gap. Most companies focus on matching and beating their rivals. Head to head competition based largely on incremental improvements in cost, quality or both. New market space is formed by creating products or service for which there are no direct competitors. Creative strategies or to think outside the box are rarely accompanied by practical advice. Creating new market space requires a different pattern of strategic thinking where looking beyond the accepted boundary of innovation helps in finding unoccupied territory that represents a real breakthrough in value. To introduce the first motivational idea in finding the innovation gap, as first introduced by Quicken, a firm should at first look at reducing the differences, like what factors should be reduced well below the industry standard?. Certain ideas like elimination of factors to create more indispensible and sustainable strategies are very important and it is very important to create an outlook that the industry has never thought of. Firms like 3M and GE have grown with that. These firms have always been aware and improved on factors that can be raised well beyond industry standards. There are many customer related factors that can be looked upon to transform this situation. Individual companies in an industry often target different customer segments- large versus small customers. But an industry typically converges on a single buyer group. Challenging an industrys conventional wisdom about which buyer group to target can lead to the discovery of new market space. There should always be an analytic sense of the capabilities that help in creating new features of product or creates the information for competitors that can help in building an analysis to headstart the future generation of innovation. Other factors that may be involved are coverage of price quotes, coverage of news, terminal ease of use, on-line analytics that helps in building the relationship and growth in the form of a pyramid. It is also very important to formalize which is more important and which is less important. In unfolding the main phenomenon behind this, it is very important to understand the untapped value which is often hidden in complementary products and services.

Companies often find new market space when they are willing to challenge the functional-emotional orientation of the industry. Stripping extras away, both from the emotional model and the practical outlook that may sustain or may not sustain helps in building simpler, lower-priced, lower-cost business model that customers would welcome. The value curve also seems to form a very important segmented image of a win-win strategy with its different components of success right from marketing to its product identification all being performed at a relative level. Similarly firms that have innumerable products should necessarily sustain in developing all its products and create different financial derivations and analysis for all of its product to reduce the value gap and increase the performance of each of its products. It is very important to focus on rivals within an industry to close the gap. This helps in creating substitute products and more often build a strong idea of creating complementary products. It also helps in building a dominance in strategic group. It helps in better serving the buyer group that depends more on individual tastes and are more oriented towards previous demands and success stories that leads to increasing the buyer group for a particular product. This past performance increases the predictability and dependability for a sustainable outlook for the future, which may sometimes look vague but maximizing the product-employee related benefits in the value curve can reduce any deficits. It helps in maximizing the price-performance and value of the products that helps to create relative understanding of the emotional orientation of the industry. This helps in understanding the necessities and the requirements.

TECHNOLOGY	PERFORMANCE	INNOVATION GAP
TRADITIONAL TECHNOLOGY	NEW MARKETS FIND IT DIFFICULT, MORE PROBABLE IN EMERGING MARKETS	PERFORMANCE ANALYSIS DIFFICULT TO KEEP ON DEVELOPING
NEW TECHNOLOGY	FINDS PREFERENCE FOR DEVELOPMENT IN NEW MARKETS	PROTOTYPES ARE REDUCED FOR SPECIFIC MARKET AND MORE DEVELOPED MARKET SHARE, WHICH SHOWS UNIQUENESS

TECHNOLOGY, PERFORMANCE AND INNOVATION
B.CHATTERJEE (2009)

It is also very necessary to understand the market trend which can be very well classified by plotting between time and people who need a new product. There is always a positive trend in every product between lead users, early adopters and routine users which all can be classified in the commercial products availability scenario. The lead users create solutions mainly in compatible products which is very critical or in user related products like medical diagnosis equipments, scanners or X-ray diffraction equipments which potentially relates to user knowledge satisfaction and his potentiality for betterment through the service engineer. Medical radiology and semiconductor imaging are a part of expert understanding.

TYPES AND INSTANCES	SUSTAINING TECHNOLOGIES	DISRUPTIVE TECHNOLOGIES
TECHNOLOGY TRANSITION	EASIER TO UNDERSTAND ITS EFFECTS AND GIVE MORE EMPHASIS ON ITS EFFECTS ON ECONOMY	DETERMINE THE MARKET NEED AND TOTALLY DEPENDS ON MARKET STAGE OR TRANSFORMATION CAPABILITY OF THE ECONOMY
MARKET POSITION	HEAVY ENGINEERING GOODS OCCUPY AN IMPORTANT POSITION AS WELL AS NANOTECHNOLOGY	CREATES A CLEAN POSITION AND A DISCRIMINATION BETWEEN THE DIFFERENT MARKETS
RESOURCE ALLOCATION	ALL THE MAJOR RESOURCES PROVIDE A CHALLENGE, A MUCH BIGGER CHALLENGE ?	CHANGE AND NEED TO BE CHANGED WITH TIME, NEEDS EXTENSIVE MATHEMATICAL AND LOGICAL CALCULATIONS

B. CHATTERJEE (2009)

Innovation gap is a scenario of uncertainty and business ideas have real commercial potential in their fraught with uncertainty. There are many challenges to solving this. A new product has to offer customers exceptional utility at an attractive price and the company must be able to deliver it at a measurable profit. There is always a buyers image that is to be maintained through a buyer utility map where the six stages of buyer experience cycle is plotted to the utility factors that is a measurement of equity and value created. On one side buyers talk of management of the product and its different components that lead to purchase, delivery, use, supplements, maintenance and disposal. Similarly early changes in promotion, customer effectiveness and environmental friendliness are also very important. It is very important to understand product needs, product delivery, product work and training and expert assistance that lead to increasing the effectiveness and measure the different product performance situations. Legal and resource protection also matters, which determines how high a price you can set without inviting in competitors with imitation products. There is always a degree of legal and resource protection, where it can be measured between high degree, medium and low with different forms and relative market volume of alternatives. Once costs and capabilities are optimized towards the cost target, which is driven by the strategic price, the company should challenge the industry standard pricing model to reach more customers and increase profitability. Although digitizing assets can reduce costs, it can bring low added value or certain increase in service functions and looking more towards inspection thus somewhat reducing the buyers interests in emerging markets , if the product is completely digitized.

When a companys resources become more mature, its abilities start more from its processes- product development, manufacturing, budgeting. It helps smaller companies tend to major market shifts better than larger ones. It helps new market applications to emerge-starting from the disruptive innovation improvement that rapidly and ultimately could address the customers in the mainstream of the market. It helps to create new organizational structure within new corporate boundaries in which new processes can be developed. It is also very important to spin out an independent organization and acquire a different organization whose processes and values closely match the requirements of the new tasks. There are many tools for organizational needs in disruptive innovation. It can be transformed into commercialization and using a heavyweight team in the existing organization. It is very important to dominate on market segments by addressing the problem each being specified at a time.

It is always said that a new paradigm of innovation is always emerging: a partnership between private enterprise and public interest produces profitable and sustainable change. It matters how much a firm is moving from corporate social responsibility to social innovation looking at all the suggested factors that improves the visual and oral characteristics of the product , as well as countrywide performance generation perspective by watching the market trends that reduces the value gap on social innovation. Looking at the R&D project and new paradigm perspectives as described in the earlier chapters, the inherent uncertainty of innovation-trying something that has never been done before- means that initial project plans are best guesses, not firm forecasts. Social innovation consists of such disruptive factors like unexpected obstacles in technology, political complexities and new opportunities. To manage these a start up is the best example which can perform better than a large organization not by means of resources or skills, but by means of resources in personal and professional leadership that helps in developing a disruptive technology that cannot be fought against or developed on. Rather this technology can help in management of self created problems and cannot be made dependant on others. Recent innovations in optic fibre is one such example of emerging technologies. Generally emerging technology and certain build ups in infrastructure designing and steel production carry this phenomenon. Clayton Christensens ideas and opinions on performance of mini mills is one such example. Sometimes many non-profit agencies are businesses that create donations for business participation in the social sector. This model actively discourages companies from taking an interest in results. Companies receive their benefits upfront from tax-write offs. It is to be understood why old models of corporate support don't create sustainable change. Models are built through various justifications and implication on organization behavior and studying the implications on developing certain creative factors that are not profit making but lead to contribution like handling the disorders in management are bringing an alignment.

Cost cutting a very important understanding of todays new technology and disruptive technology. It is said that it affects everything from the development process itself- including an way in which R&D organization is structured. To improve the measurement on this a rapid experimentation is structured, which would avoid mistakes; anticipate and exploit early information; and combine new and old technologies. It is true that computer simulations, rapid prototyping allow companies to create more learning more rapidly and that knowledge can create more experiments in less expense. It is true that the derivation of knowledge management is applicable everywhere, knowledge helps in combining all the previous factors and gives a clear focus to understand the applications of any knowledge oriented subject and doesn't leave behind any barriers giving a much sharper outlook. Information based technologies have driven down the marginal costs of experimentation just as they have decreased the marginal costs in production systems. Sometimes a systems performance is jointly optimized that helps in designing the performance outlook that leaves behind all the remnants to design, build, test and analyze an experiment, after the filtration is done regarding the communication process of starting the work and the middle results and recognition of the work.

It is considered that success often makes change difficult when the image is so well defined through awards that the outside environmental factors cannot immobilize the firms growth. Immediate change becomes impossible and the firm has to look only towards changing operational and production goals rather than depending on a very stable management structure. It should be that process change is always obvious with continuous innovation in big firms and rapid evolution of new technology. Continuous experimentation takes away the ill effect of prototypes and leaves behind a more effective organization where the innovator can continuously start from scratch and develop a self sufficiency in designing , planning

, co-creation and development. To look forward towards the innovation gap, the innovator also has to look towards the performance gap where new and established technologies can bring the stable benefits of experimentation, thus building cheaper and better products with a faster and more creative ability to manipulate and perform. Savings derived from combining traditional and new technologies help in carefully understanding the organizational boundaries and revamp entrenched routines.

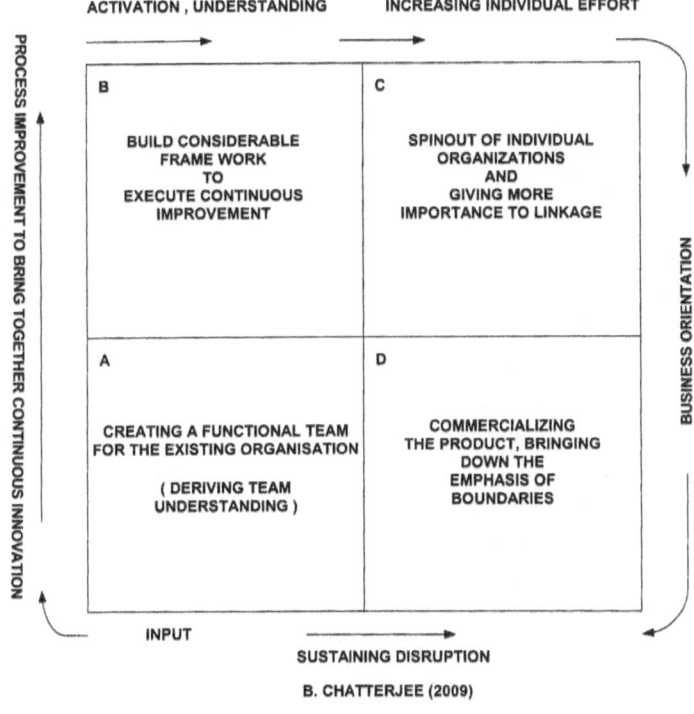

B. CHATTERJEE (2009)

If someone looks at the market perspective generally firms with disruptive technology target markets with credentials better than that of the emerging market, or highly specialized markets and firms try to target emerging markets with simple technology. Customers in these established markets eventually embraced the new architecture they had rejected earlier, because once their needs for capacity and speed were met, slowly the size of the architectural design is reduced and its complexities are also reduced making it easier to use and increasing its processing speed. As the Intel microprocessor which kept on developing and getting better on a particular aspect or single important idea to deal with. This helps process to get faster, thus developing other channels. It is very important to focus on necessary resources and capabilities to overcome the technological and organizational hurdles that impede innovation. Entrant firms have an attackers advantage over established firms in those innovations- generally new product architectures, involving little new technology per se-that disrupt or redefine the level rate. Successful entrants always finds a new market that values the technology whereas established firms attempt to push the technology in existing markets. Generally these firms always look at a very specific model for profitability that help in understanding the basic functional factors and incorporating them together to stay in the mainstream business.

Higher performance products are targeted at the larger, higher margin markets immediately above them always got resources. Sensible resource allocation processes were at the root and are the cause of a firms upward mobility. They generally occur after the company has made full investment in product design and manufacturing. In the development resources, projects targeted at the explicit needs of current customers or at needs of existing users that a supplier has not yet been able to reach will always win over products for markets that do not exist, the major priority to make this happen is the designing of the resource allocation system.

To talk more about the disruptive minimill steel technology, the integrated steel makers were experiencing dramatically improving profits, because they always depended on manufacturing the highest quality products. They utilized some of the resources of the mainstream organization to address the disruption, but they were careful not to leverage its processes and values. They created different ways of working within an organization whose values and cost structure were turned to the disruptive task at hand. New markets always value the output rather than breakthrough technology. The different strategies that influence massive reorganization are technology strategies, with which at the bottom they use proven technologies in initial products and those at top use component technologies.

Disruptive technology often enable something to be done that previously had been deemed impossible. As emerging markets are small, the organizations competing in them must be able to become profitable at small scale. Large organizations need not necessarily allocate freely the necessary financial and human resources needed to build a strong position in emerging markets. When a threatened disruptive technology requires a different cost structure in order to be profitable and competitive, or when the current size of the opportunity is insignificant relative to the growth of the mainstream organization, then there needs to be a possible spinout.

To quote as stated before regarding the competitive battles and as stated above regarding the structure and success of the minimills one of the most predictable events is that after establishing an initial foothold, new firms experience a strong incentive to improve, acquire more customers and migrate into high-profit tiers of their market. The signals of change consists of elaborating on the different customer types: undershot customers, nonconsumers, nonmarket contexts and overshot customers. It is very important to analyze the likely results of the head to head battles and its strengths and weaknesses. Differentiation strategy helps a firm search for new markets that value for points of differentiation. Only by moving up into new markets can firms sustain these advantages.

It is very important to understand potentially disruptive innovation where performance and time are the key factors and to deal with that the major challenges are developing on the technology infrastructure of small market satisfied with not-good-enough functionality in exchange for other benefits and depend on large market by moving ahead taking the major components of both to develop on good functionality even if it is found that good functionality is intolerable. Co-option is a very important choice in todays business, growth driven co-option needs to occur early and entails going after an entrant's core customers. It is very important to understand whether the firm can create a perfect and right foothold with the perfect disruptive strategy. To understand the forces of disruptive technology for the new entrant firms the firm has to better study the value networks.

Market signals are becoming a key priority for strategy making where there are limited fixed-cost infrastructure that encourages experimentation, demonstrate willingness to adapt to market signals, and develops business plans that tests rather than assumes. There are many new entrants looking for a target, they are mainly firms constrained in accessing resources or reaching potential customers and have to create a specific channel and new networking and communications model , to turn it into a profitable business.

To improve the creation of products and services and bring a uniqueness in the products and move up-market, these providers need to overcome some serious technological challenges. Issues related to limited distance such as the technology's range, presence management and security all make crafting a profitable business model challenging. It is always very important to focus on the important analytical processes signals of change, competitive battles and strategic choices that helps in describing the different broad business to develop on.

It is very important to understand the disruptive models on innovation to work on. The first of them would be built on pace of technological progress built on the ability to develop on sustaining innovations all derived on performance that customers can utilize or absorb . All these are dependant on range of performance that customers can utilize. It is very important to depend on low-end disruption that addresses overserved customers with a lower cost business model. It is also very important to emphasize on new market disruptions that compete against nonconsumption, all these depending on sustainable strategy that helps in bringing a better product into an established market. New market disruptions make the incumbents face lesser threat until the final stages. It is good for leading firms because for a time they are replacing the low-margin revenues that disruptors steal, with higher margin revenues from sustaining innovations. To put an emphasis on value gap and innovation gap, it is also found that a performance gap is created through it. The main forces for diminishing this performance gap is by beating competitors with functionality and reliability, using performance and balanced scorecard measures to generate speed and responsiveness. This helps in maximizing the benefits and optimizing the situation. To understand the locus of advantage it is very important to concentrate on interdependent design and assembly putting lesser focus on sourcing of parts. It is also very important to look at the direct and interdependent manufacturer-customer interface. The usual processes are not the only value added processes involved in logistics, development, manufacturing and customer service. The other processes are depending on the previous talked about factors including legal factors for investment decisions. It is very important to understand the organizations values and collaborate them with deliberate strategy, emergent strategy, investments in the different credentials and units of management and the fundamental decisions of a corporate as well as look at the resource allocation process, where it is very important to look at what works and what doesn't as well as look at the problems and success.

Creation of new disruptive businesses that allows companies to exceed investor expectations and create unusual shareholder value. The idea channels those that need something to fuel their own disruptive march-up market against their competition also become unattractive. To conclude we have to say that potentially disruptive businesses are small, but their ill-defined strategies and demanding profitability targets, make-or-break decisions arise with alarming frequency, and such businesses have no processes for making these decisions correctly whereas larger businesses have greater customer needs and clearly articulated needs. To overcome this problem the firm has to concentrate more on the value gap as discussed earlier, as well as resources, logistics and leadership that can be well understood through understanding market signals and understanding the competitive battles.

Chapter 8

(Baisham Chatterjee student UNBSJ) Further analysis on sustaining and disruptive technologies

Any form of technology are the processes including marketing, investment and managerial process and engineering and manufacturing. It is a combination of all these that transforms labour, capital, materials and information. Many designing firms specializing with machinery and tool designing stay stable and need not change until the need is required to change the machinery which has been recognized for a particular purpose. These technologies very often stay in the market for a long time like various kinds of X-Ray diffractometer, excavators, hydraulic breaks, machinery etc. They result in developing improved performance in established products and thus transforms the idea of discontinuous innovation giving it a sustainable outlook. To focus at the customers wish list the major challenges are sustainable technology improvements over the minimum product performance required which is calculated by the price/value gap that creates a major switch in the market requirements, segmentation and target market. All the relations and perceptual and logical derivations are based on the minimum product performance required as well as the credibility gap new technologies have to cross and the time and the logical thought process involved during the production planning that can help new technologies break into the mainstream. It is always said that new entrants that take up the disruptive technology are able to gain an unassailable advantage. What might be seen as a niche market is where the next phase of rapid industry growth would occur.

A company will commit considerable investment to projects, however technologically risky if its customers want and need the resulting products. Large companies should hive off their own disruptive technology projects into fledgling organizations that can be excited by the opportunities afforded by small markets. It avoids distraction as it pursues growth via sustaining technologies. It is said that according to Christensen's research learning and discovery of markets is always very important. Factors that not only help in creating disruptive technology solutions but help to build on it are through people, equipment, product design, brands, information etc. Technology helps in improving performance in different products and similarly low-cost products can give high returns. It is always said : talk to the customers first.

Business intelligence in innovation that gives the different results of creating separate disruptive technology profiles, are by: generating ideas that form the key base of the technology, forming clusters within and outside the firm, describe technologies and disruptions, screen disruptive technologies according to client criteria, based on the different criticalities of business, their markets, and the technology base on which they depend. This gives the correct result of how to develop more credible source, and keep on generating further new ideas through it. Sometimes key technology news articles and information centres form an important source.

Biogerontechnology has a broad base of stakeholders committed to advancing biomedical research and is an ultimate stage of disruptive technology:

- Public-policy interest groups will seek to influence legislation controlling regulation of and access to

biogerontechnology. Similarly environmentalists might question the societal value of biogerontechnology relative to that of other population and sustainability challenges. Social advocates might be motivated to raise public consciousness of issues that deal with the impacts on this disruptive technology on attitudes and evolution.
- There are various issues and uncertainties of this research starting from commercialization of this biomedical technology, implementing this and evolution of further results through research and implementing strong policy and regulatory framework to restrict and control interdisciplinary research environments, human research validation (including genetic research that should have certain and deliberate government force and measures to limit the research), clinical development and applications is another key source.

Another form of disruptive technology is an alternative to conventional lithography or imprint patterning: that is a novel method for producing high density interconnects. The most important method of imprint patterning is its cost resistance and effectiveness because it eliminates many of the traditional front-end process steps typically utilized when patterning structures with photoresists. Dexter-Loctite Corp and Ormet Corp are two such very creative firms in the United States that brought into view this disruptive technology. It is taken to be an alternative process for producing interconnects in both PCB and IC packaging applications. DSSP (digital shape sampling and processing) a disruptive technology innovation helps in 3D scanning and digital processing to coordinate points by the society of manufacturing engineers. It helps in product definition to measurement process definition, measurement process execution to analysis and reporting. They all consist of various parts starting from create part geometry, defining features, defining tolerances, identifying resources, define setup, define sensor, identify measurements, collect ,load and manipulate data as well as retrieve data , analyze , measurements to see whether the product passes the test. Digital shape sampling helps in loading a new part of data, scanning the part, compare the part design with CAD and then looking at the measurement whether it would be pass or fail. If the product test fails then the failed characteristics should be identified. Similarly the disruptive technology brought out by Philips is known as Access Point. It is also known as information when you need it and where you need it. The disruptive technology in the case of Access Point is the AP communicator- a voice-controlled internet browser that forms the heart of the Access Point System. As voice-recognition algorithms improve, the spoken word may become the main interface to the internet. Access Point is an integrated, single-supplier solution provider of just-in-time information. It is an aligned and collectively shared value proposition that addresses the application and its multiple set of stakeholders must drive the choice of network partners and collective strategy formulation. Knowledge is a key factor of production in Access Points networks. One of the key strategic challenges faced by Access Point and its network involves the rapid absorption and integration of new knowledge with old as well as the reconfiguration of that knowledge into new business opportunities. Knowledge is equal to sum of people to information at the power of sharing.

Disruptive technology very often faces a major strategic risk which has to have countermeasures. Such risks are like inability to understand technology, brand collapse, one of-a-kind competitor and industry economics collapse. Certain disruptive ideas can show customer shift, stagnation of previous business because of predetermination. Other risks involved are double betting, continuous measurement, crisis management, early warning system of the disruptive technology that can divert the firms business, complete change. To help disruptive technologies occur, it is necessary to share information and asset based on the required and power of the disruptive technology.

It is said that disruptive innovations now tend to occur at the intersection of market insight and technological know-how, making technology an input to the strategy process rather than an after-the-fact enabler. There are many factors that guide scale of entry strategies and market selection. Innovative companies often look at breaking these rules-often leveraging technology to deliver profit at a lower scale point or achieve an unexisted advantage. Innovative companies often or constantly are seeking out alternative business models that have the ability to disrupt or undermine the incumbent industry business model. Technology plays a pivotal role, allowing a business model to emerge that does not rely on historical operating model or profit mechanisms, often shifting large amounts of market value to the innovative competitor. It also helps in speeding time to market and reduces risk of technology obsolescence. The main plan behind building a disruptive technology is developing the prototype into designing it, building it and then launching it to operate. The main disruptive focus is created when the product is rebuilt and then relaunched.

The increasing complexity and market economics create a substantial knowledge gap between theory and practice. Many companies are not organized to give new ideas a chance or adapt quickly to changing market situations or even if they adapt to the changing situations the firms product line is not strong enough with creativity to target a new market or control competition. This is when disruptive technologies come into view with breakthrough innovations and disruptive business concepts, that can change the creative nature and position of new technology. It is true that the nature of customers in the modern world lead to understanding the nature of business they have to be in, the competition in which they have to survive that lead to developing the internal factors through its competencies and resources that lead to radical innovation. The main inputs and constituents behind disruptive innovation are problem identification, facts finding, problem definition, ideas development, optimizing the experiment, concept definition, innovation development plan, plan acceptance, prototyping and testing and implementing the new idea. The downstream component of radical innovation refers to the market side, things such as market acceptance, available distribution channels, alliances and external infrastructure. It is a situation where the competence can be understood in developing existing successful products, develop successful business model which would lead to lacking organizational dualism, excessive bureaucracy, path dependency & dominant design. High risk and uncertainty and learning gap form an additional key strategy issues in an organization. This leads to risk adverse climate and unwilling to cannibalise own investment. Creativity can be covered up in value innovation by market sensing and resource calculation and maximizing its utilization. Other factors involved behind this are senior management outlook and talent that can continuously improve innovation process.

Similarly E-commerce is a disruptive technology and there are streams of technological innovation to improve these key performance attributes for the disruptive technology. The different forms of disruptive technology are the streams of incremental innovation in certificate signature technologies will eventually replace the current secure socket layer technology to improve online transaction security. Sustaining innovations will raise each attributes performance along steep trajectory to quickly satisfy the needs of mainstream customers. E-commerce can be termed to be a disruptive technology because of five steps: redefining competitive advantage, rethinking business strategy in ways as defined by use of Web, re-examine traditional business and revenue models, re-engineer the corporation and web site, re-invent customer service.

Introducing disruptive technology has a lot of technology problems. It involves the creation of a system that puts into actual operations management's solution to the entrepreneurial problem. The creation of such a system requires management to select appropriate technologies for manufacturing and distribution of the product or services, and to form new information, communication and control linkages. Technology cycle consists of incremental improvement, technological discontinuity, ferment and dominant design. There is something known as the S-curve that has been talked about earlier. The technology changes from one S-curve to another needs to be discontinuous. The discrimination or differentiation between the technology change and technology exploitation of mature technologies deals with the technology base that has been derived from utilization of resources, availability of power or entrepreneurship to bring out the change and ability to derive technology and business models that can together form a very supportive combination to generate potential disruptive image and set a more control and technique oriented goal. There are many changes along the S-curve. Sustainable changes continue along the same basic pattern as measured by the same performance measures, whereas disruptive changes start an entirely new S-curve that needs to be measured by another performance parameter. Technology investment distinguishes between monitoring/early adoption, selectively investing/follower, developing key technology, maintaining mature technology and divesting of obsolete technology as the life cycle nears another technology shift. Disruptive technological change is becoming more prominent way of overcoming competitive battles and leadership efforts forces by large organizations. Stable technological change cannot bring any determination or coordination plans between what has to be done in the far future. It is somewhat difficult to remove the market and innovation gap which disruptive technology can somewhat although disruptive technology tends towards creating new markets and increase revenues abruptly.

In the situation of sustainable change, it is necessary to innovate faster and constantly. There is no focus on product and process innovation and not on administrative innovation. For instance, portfolio methods, technology planning and many others have been found in the two cases of technology exploitation and sustainable technology changes.

Very frequently in his work Christensen has talked about cannibalization. It is the pursuit of a deliberate, ongoing strategy of developing new products and processes that will attract buyers of existing products or replace existing processes of the same firm. Similarly in the proactive cannibalization process existing technology is transferred to customer value requirements and then to proactive cannibalization which can be categorized into two parts value migration strategy and incremental innovation. value migration refers to replacement of the existing product by the value offering of a discontinuous technology. Digital technology disrupts conventional photography. Christensen points out the dangers of disruptive technology. The initial value offerings based on disruptive technology may be prohibitive in cost and lower in quality compared to existing products. It may also develop into future threats by abandoning a technology that seems vague or not so well improved on, but would not vanish and do better in the long run. Very often it is found that disruptive threat possesses a negative effect on sustainable technology. This is because sustainable technology does not change very often as taken up by large corporations, but disruptive firms are generally found to be SMEs or very large scale organizations in Europe that can not only have the ability to generate huge market expansion plans but can also create technology hubs for any future development based on the same product as practiced by Grundfos of Denmark. This is a base plan brought about by making resource commitments, leveraging capabilities and building a development process right from scratch involving all the strategy tools.

THE CHANGE IN COMPETITION OF DISRUPTIVE TECHNOLOGY

PUSH UP MARKET TOWARDS HIGHER-END CUSTOMERS	STAY WITH CUSTOMERS	CHANGE THE MARKET'S DEMAND FOR FUNCTIONALITY
- Performance seems to increase as Technology becomes more prominent and keeps on changing with time. - Not very reliable because it depends on size of Target Market.	- Based on customers focus and acceptance - Customers find it based on their understanding experience and knowledge - Customers feel the disruptive technology to be a major brand focus, based on R & D Experimentation. - Price is based on discrete factors like segmented market, Probability of further change in product design and ability to succeed.	- Depends on Market conditions, entrants, exits and performance of new products. - The technology lag of closing the innovation gap makes it clearer. - Seems to depend on collaborative image as well as Customer focus.

B. CHATTERJEE (2009)

With emergence and convergence technologies that are sustaining in nature, most established companies are adept at turning these into achievements. Relational assets and networks have set ways in approaching new technologies. They also remain steadfast to their existing webs of relationships, by pushing the barriers of existing technology. Disruptive technologies in particular have a potentiality of a very high revenue earner but may lack an effective CRM or customer interaction, declining margins and lost opportunity. Business models of established telecommunication carriers are a convergence of information technology and telecommunication services and products and business solutions leads to a shift in the adoption of these carriers business models.

There are many challenges of emerging and converging technologies:

- Investments are complicated by the difficulties in forecasting the pace of emerging and converging technologies and the rate of marketing acceptance, operating within the current set of performance standards or technology barriers.
- Rapid technology progression causes major disruption to existing technology standards, reconfigure the industry value chain, create single market and network and numerous sub-markets. Thus making disruptive technology the major impact creators in modern business is by dealing with the specialities of a single product or a single technological aspect.
- Industrial procurement and supply chain activities, partnerships, alliances and acquisition targets will no longer be limited to be known, by established companies in the value chain.
- Firms take a portfolio stake via a series of value chain integration activities. It is difficult to invest businesses in the value chain who are willing to concentrate on the internal credentials of the value chain as a measure of the changing technology landscape.

The most critical strategic decisions many companies face today is to figure out what role they play when their markets are disrupted. In telecommunications, computers and software firms with perpetual disruption, this is very urgent. So instead of launching creative new products these companies should launch creative new structures. Printing too is today a disruptive technology where the factors employees depend on are not employees of the large corporations-they are independent contractors who feed their products into the large corporations distribution channels. In the new disruptive model new-to-the-world product development would come from venture-capital-backed startups. They spinout startups into breakthrough technologies and once a stratup has proven a concept, rights of product are sold to large distribution companies who will sell it and service it worldwide.

There are many value proposition trends which start from the market consisting of opponents that are the competitors partners, to the value proposition that has a high level vision to product level goals to end to end scenarios to feature level design to projects management dependencies scheduling which leads to lastly bringing a breakthrough idea from these decision flows.

Another very important idea we deal with today is open innovation that focuses more on R&D in large organizations. Dissimilarly disruptive technology focuses at developing on ideas of SMEs and firms that deal more with breakthrough technology developments.

Chapter 9

(Baisham Chatterjee student UNBSJ)
Alliances in innovation for product development

Alliances in innovation creates extended innovation and is used in mature industries in which the competitive structure has long remained unchanged or is highly consolidated. Moreover when a firm looks towards increasing its business prospects, it looks towards concentrating on the emerging spaces in which the competitive structure and industry dynamics have yet to crystallize. Alliances both in technology agreements and licensing look at disaggregation of business units to focus on its most challenging capabilities such as innovation. It is said that firms that have a cross-industry knowledge are more likely to innovate.

Inter-firm cooperative arrangements are the key success factors in bringing coordination and better knowledge prospects to increase innovation. Strategic alliances always deal with mutual strategic objectives and emerge as a response to shifting patterns of market competition and intense pressure for rapid technological innovation. Mobide is recently known to be a very successful inter-firm strategy framework that emerges through R&D collaboration. Strategic alliances help firms to proceed in the launching of their product or service into the market and enter into an entirely new challenging phase. To elaborate on this inter-firm level process the collaboration should initiate this by means of finding the right fit and establish rules of interaction. After that the firm should use configuration techniques by establishing a strong sense of control and conflict management. After that the firm should establish performance measures. The final rules are stabilizing the expectations by bringing the balance between the initial processes that are configured, then reconfigured and then implemented. Such processes are to be stabilized for constantly creating a new performance platform for new R&D collaborations. The final stage seeks at transformation that can sense new market demands and searches for market newness and more advanced but easy to contribute in markets. Mobide's action plans for the commercialization phase are based on the alliance management framework. The Mobides strategic alliance consists of roles that will be needed for a fully operational alliance, which consists of:

- Content owner that can be various entities like municipalities or newspapers who will sell their content to the alliance.
- Content providers role would be undertaken either by each city that buys the service or by a single company that will have the responsibility to collect all the necessary content for the service.
- Wireless applications service provider is the third step and once the technological solution is developed, the academic developer would withdraw and industrial developer would undertake the management and maintenance.
- The fourth and the last is the network operator that is integrated in the bouquet of offers of mobile service providers.

In this type of alliance perspective it is very necessary to facilitate a long-term collaboration that would help to organize frequent meetings with partners during innovation to introduce the idea of a common alliance. Moreover to spread the idea of an extensive R&D the firm has to promote the idea of alliance, commercialize it and decide upon that. After this is done, it is very important to identify the alliance champion and in many cases, an inter-firm arrangement is not seen from inception as a potential alliance. This alliance champion must be identified early in any intervention effort: and for this measure the alliance has to be promoted. It is very important to identify alliance roles for the commercialization phase , which would make it easier to understand technology and bring a closer mindset between technology and networking with industries, individuals and focus groups.

It is very often said that corporate's are a lifelong learning environment where strategic business units, business schools and universities with self developed or government funded research centre's, consultants that creates specialist development providers as well as supply chains that are more probable to succeed within a shared territory or bridge a learning venture or development venture to communicate and bring together research and learning. The alliance structure helps the government draft ideas, carry out learning needs, look at strategic learning objectives and look at alliance relationship, as well as partners alliance structure, systems, responsibilities, desired outcome. Practice management is a automatically derived criteria that starts after the basic relationship is created.

Innovation has become very prominent in high velocity industries where the level of competitive rivalry among firms is high. Thus high velocity industries-biotechnology, computers, electronics, semiconductors and telecommunications- have experienced a boom in R&D activities during the past decade. This affects the development as well as the learning opportunities of member firms. Notwithstanding the potential for knowledge creation and innovation in technology alliances, collaborative learning in alliances happens over time as their alliances evolve. It is said that technology alliances share R&D

costs. This is because firms in industries with a high cost of R&D are more likely to seek consortia as a cost sharing mechanism. Innovation types are defined into operational dealing with the core processes and products, services and markets. Sometimes it happens that it is important to identify the potentials and importance of global connectivity, created through telecommunications, IT infrastructure and open standards that enables entirely new forms of collaboration and thus new business models. This reduces collaboration and transaction costs, companies are taking advantage of the expertise and scale that lies hidden in their own organizations and across the globe. This enables shared services centres to develop specialized capabilities to create truly differentiating business designs.

An innovators business models can be created in various ways, starting from various capabilities and implementations of the product for cost reduction, strategic flexibility and assessments of various strategy implementations, focus and specialization, rapidly exploit new markets to provide opportunities to new products. (this is sometimes difficult as markets may have variable risk factors starting from consumption in low market ends or spreading the tactics of branding in the middle, it is all but very time taking and requires a lot of heart.) It is also very necessary to move from fixed to variable cost in this situation.

It has been observed that there has been a clear pattern of growth in the R&D partnerships in the economy. This is due to increased scientific and technological complexity, higher uncertainty surrounding R&D, increased costs of R&D projects and shortened innovation cycles that favor collaboration. These partnerships help to learn and develop company activities across the value chain. High tech sectors help in measuring and reorganizing the different dimensions in the competitive landscape which may be reoriented in 5 dimensions: highly competitive with huge focus on R&D,

competitive with focus on business interests and depending on prototypes for improvement, average (firms depending on R&D as well as business interests), not so competitive(that focus on other markets, with their personal markets becoming very vulnerable. Such businesses have a huge risk factor and their products often fail in the market.), unsuccessful businesses (businesses that fail and don't carry any leadership and focus for growth or skills to develop R&D). Co-opetition is another human created factor that can save this ill effects. It may be encouraged by public R&D-funding and the desire to share substantial costs and risks in the case of products based on technological breakthroughs. Product innovation generates revenues, process innovation helps in safeguarding and improving quality and for saving costs. Market innovation is concerned with improving mix of target markets and how chosen markets are best served. Radical innovation is a new product or system with original state-of-art proprietary technology that will significant expand the capabilities of existing ones. It requires significant R&D. Intermediate innovation is a new product with proprietary technology however it may be duplicated by others. Significant incremental innovation refers to significant extension of product characteristics with original adaptation of available technology. Meanwhile after we look at technical integration, innovation processes and strategic technology planning, we talk of technology integration. This integrates technology and the product-markets of the firm emphasizes the importance of satisfying the customer with the innovations of the firm.

Very often we talk of the term open innovation by focusing the relationships between universities and firms as a vehicle for acquiring technological knowledge. High technology and rapidly changing industries requires huge amount of R&D investment and are associated with high risk. As a consequence firms in high-tech industries correspond more with other firms. Overall firms that are able to rapidly access fresh, new knowledge and integrate it into their current processes are more likely to enjoy a competitive advantage. The quest for this competitive advantage is leading firms to partially outsource their research processes in order to increase efficiency and efficacy and to secure a critical mass of technological knowhow. Open innovation is considered as a crucial factor for managing knowledge flows is considered crucial for competition. It is said that there are three main characteristics of companies that cooperate effectively. The first stage are related to innovators, second stage is related to cutting edge of technology, involving high levels of uncertainty regarding technology. There is often innovation and research associated with specific collaborations that are undertaken by the research director.

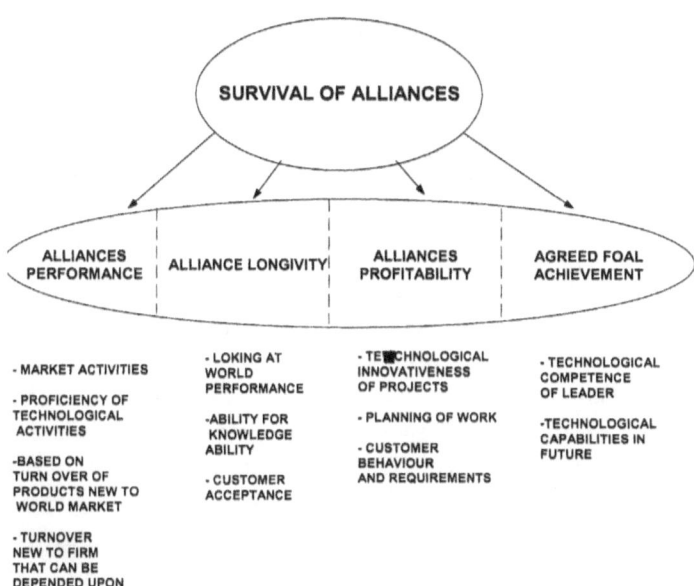

To produce rapid innovation, Japanese companies have learned to manage strategic communities for new product development. These communities require the merging and integration of different technologies and the coordination of relationships among all levels of management, alliance partners and customers. Networking strategic communities as in Fujitsu is done by means of communications, customer and by bringing a domestic and overseas outlook of manufacturers of a particular product that integrate together and bring a coordination between the most important to the least important five types of strategic communities that affect and are related to the network divison. The first 4 type of strategic communities are related to traditional organizations, corporate users, suppliers that help in developing and comparing the relationship and internal communication of different competitors and how they relate to each other according to their base technology. The studies for synthesis were linked to 4 distinct areas: based on value of employees possessing a broad diversity of viewpoints that are shaped by the knowledge of corporate cultures. Integrating system technology elements help in diffusing among the different strategic communities and it is also very important to balance different business models. Dialectical leadership, synthesizing capability and new knowledge creation are the three very important knowledge creative abilities solely focused on the leadership factors like creative leadership and strategic leadership.

In this situation of continuous change, there is no dominant design to build on and technology, the market and competition are difficult to predict. Different innovations compete to become the dominant design, making innovation management an activity dealing with large amounts of uncertainty. In obtaining the resources like knowledge of technology and market, management capabilities, distribution and production skills to ensure a strong support of resource allocation and power struggles, the factor involved over here is known as product champion. It is a person or team strongly connected with the innovation, prepared to defend and argue for it in times of tough questions and it needs a product sponsor. To bring a strong relationship of a product sponsor and a product a various degree of structural level has been designed. It consists of exploring a certain product or a service innovation or a critical subsystem, developing prototypes and small-scale live experiments in order to test the validity of product/service concepts, all these brought out by idea generations and a strong foundation built in the hierarchy level.

New product development needs a lot of attention in its independent development factors like network set-up factors, network coordination factors and dependant variables and measures. New product development can be reinforced through procedures like customer involvement, supplier involvement, marketing and technological synergy, internal/external communication, senior management support, product advantage and proficiencies of pre-development activities as well as many financial variables that varies on a year on year basis. It is very necessary to look at the survival of alliances by looking at all the in depth factors that increases the growth potentiality beyond a given time frame.

It has been derived that there are few principles that are important in sub-contracting or other purposes like: accessing technology, specialist skills and knowledge; allow firms to focus on core activities; access better costs through sub-contractors economy of scales; access to investment in supply chain. In R&D collaborations it is always very necessary to maintain long term relations. Along with these relations high costs of change regularly occur and are considered strategic. Asset specificity frequently exists and greatly influences the cost and ease of change. Relationships are often viewed as dynamic exchanges and not as simple transactions. Technology driven, sharing of resources, asset specific investments possess high ability of collaborations that can bring high volume exchanges. Two major reasons behind competitors collaborating on R&D alliances are the financial requirement involved and the desire to jointly establish new industry standard but all are not based on solid economic grounds. Many alliances are based on trend settings. Strategic alliances have direct impact on the firm evaluation. Alliances including joint ventures and other product-market relationship among firms, are found to be associated with significant increases in stock market performance, investment and operating profitability especially those requiring high levels of research. In order to increase the value proposition and its applications, the firm has look at:

- Creating new value by delivering a broad range of goods and services, increasing its quality, accessing innovation and incorporating into product offer and facilitating new product development.
- Out of the three major challenges the third one is building current business capability which consists of building the right kind of expertise through training, accessing resources, building finance capability, and building all the logistics capabilities consisting of distribution, manufacturing and purchasing.
- The last important idea behind this is defending market position that is a critical asset of building a successful R&D, which consists of building barriers against new entrants, competing against major chains, offset impact of product substitutes and defending against environmental forces. These three factors show the major intent and challenges to be reorganized for making a successful strategic alliance in an R&D.

Strategic alliances also look at knowledge transfer, between partners and depends on the nature of knowledge that is to be created and managed. Complex knowledge and tacit knowledge, core knowledge and relationship and protection which all can be transferred into non-core knowledge and make knowledge more related and simple through many teamwork and group skills , as well as bringing and designing a proper technology to bring this idea into action.

To offset the foregone benefits of economies of scale and scope, which are enjoyed by large firms by virtue of their size and coverage, small firms create strategic alliances aiming at leveraging each others strengths and competence. Leading business strategists promote the idea of developing networks among firms to strengthen their competitiveness. Such networks will involve much cooperation and reciprocity between the participants across boundaries. Inter-firm arrangements are very important and its arrangements include cost sharing, technology transfer and sharing of information. Among the characteristics that make a firm a desirable alliance partner are having financial resources, technological know-how, market position, reputation or unique managerial or human resources. Providing knowledge-based services through the correct investments and problem solving factors enhance learning that helps to obtain a strong financial return and hence also increase the knowledge base.

Many a time it is found that market globalization transforms the nature of corporate operations. Competitive and strategic advantages now derives from companies capacities to cooperate with other firms; to form business network models with suppliers and buyers; to reap economies of scale; and to share costs and benefits with culturally distinct locations. Globalization forces are the key drivers forcing corporations to explore alternative ways of preserving and gaining competitive advantage. Shorter product life-cycles and rapid technological change and increased demand for global firms for systematic solutions. Moreover R&D collaborations typically require mutual experiential learning activities to synthesize original knowledge, which then becomes the venture owners joint intellectual property. Whether organizational learning involves acquiring routine or extraordinary knowledge, transaction cost analysts caution that alliance participants risk potential opportunism from their unrestricted access to proprietary secrets and unrestricted processes. Repeated R&D

collaborations creates mutual learning processes and are more related to organizational ethics to protect the firm from getting ripped off. Innovation and sales rates increased substantially if a firm was connected to more technologically innovative and revenue rich alliance partners. Firms that transfer proprietary knowledge and pool specialized resources and employee skills into a joint R&D project that sometimes achieve technological breakthroughs with widespread product applications that yield huge market capacity for co-creating a market potentiality of the firm as well as all its related partners.

In contrast to mature and stable environment where uncertainty of the environment if any is considered low, R&D collaborations are challenged in emerging technology based industries are characterized by high uncertainty, due to different and sudden technological evolution, market volatility and competition unpredictability. There are 7 dimensions in a research framework. The first being strategic factors consisting of fast follower and cost minimization. The other important point is the alliance orientation factors consisting of technology absorption that depends more on innovation skills and understanding ability, technology risk reduction orientation, and R&D scale economy orientation. Alliance capability factors consists of previous expertise and technology adaptation and learning capabilities. The 4th is technology alliance model consisting of joint development and licensing agreement. They all together combine to relate to strategic resources that consist of technology, product and process management capabilities. The other key factors that help in building an alliance are quality management competence and technology competence. All these factors when they work out together define the overall business performance.

Organizational strategies are generally technology oriented and focus on innovation and growth. Most organizations are functionally organized. Organizational strategies generally focus on growth, to attain economies of scale and on diversification to reduce financial risks. Many organizations adopt a multi-divisional structure. Technology science push is also an important factor. The process of commercialization of technology is perceived as a linear progression from scientific discovery to the market place. Many R&D departments are staff departments that are structured like scientific institutions. There is also need of a market pull in this next generation innovation collaboration models, where technological change is rationalized, needs are considered more important to innovation than scientific and technological progress. These R&D collaborations can be vastly read into broadly three different types and are brought together on basis of linkage between: new to the market, new to the company and new to the technology. It requires different R&D management practices, in case of cooperation between R&D and marketing departments. Service development processes very often has a similarity with product development processes. Small firms rely more heavily on informal than on formal in-house R&D and use outside sources of knowledge less frequently than larger firms, reflecting their limited capacity to absorb outside knowledge. Thus in small firms modes of innovation are dependant on firms competencies, business opportunities and managerial preferences.

Regardless of the lack of theory to explain such choices, firms are willing to expend considerably more effort in managing the transactions between themselves and their key suppliers in hopes of gaining more than the specified goods or services- such benefits as quality improvement, technical assistance and competitive advantage. These advantages may only be available from some supplier relationships. Without the effect of suppliers input there may be no fertile ground for developing alliance relationship. Their research in several fields are as:

- There should be a match in the organizational and strategic objectives of the buyer and supplier firms. A match in values or philosophies held by buyer and

supplier firms and develop purchasing relationships. Develop a collaborative idea to develop technical resources that would help in problem solving.
- Develop planning and performance information and belief in the collaborative approach as well as share benefits with the alliances in an equitable manner.

Alliance helps firms to get fast access to technology, knowledge and skills located outside organizational boundaries and increase economies of scale by pooling resources. It helps share risks for costly projects that exceed the affordability of a single firm. There are many uncertainties involved in alliances, which are as: processes by which firms select partners and form alliances, contents of selection of uncertainty and mechanisms for reducing selection of uncertainty. It is very necessary to define opportunities that would help in developing technological competence of prospective partners and potential commercial success of proposing alliances. Competitive benchmarking and putting more light on new product development and R&D that helps in transforming resources and putting a further emphasis on new product revenues and innovation that are positively linked to performance. It is also very necessary to bring in supply chains and use it as a measure of collaboration, which can be done by means of: collaborative management, virtual collaboration and vertical, horizontal and lateral integration. But supply chains can bear a great importance in modifying the problem of uncertainty and create a major impact in lessening the bridge between time- environment-technology logic and creation, that can prove and negate the dissimilarities in uncertainty.

Chapter 10

(Baisham Chatterjee student UNBSJ)
High impact businesses: providing vision and focus

For looking at a higher impact the features required are more sales revenue, highest acceptable price, large market share, less material cost and less operating cost. A continuous processing of information between and within four distinct domains: consumer domain, functional domain, physical domain and process domain. The needs of the customer are established in the customer domain and then formalized in the functional domain as a set of functional requirements that bring in the main idea of the solution process. The design parameters in the physical domain are then mapped in the process domain in terms of the process variables. Greatest impact can be created through technological breakthroughs, that can create a new product as well as a new demand, creating markets that had not previously existed. Moreover the product development process has to be corrected with time and moves forward continuously. When the first round of design process is completed, it is highly probable that the additional insight gained through the first iteration may enable the designer to come up with a better set of FRs, which may in turn enable the design and manufacture of more advanced products. The availability of advanced products may then change marketing strategy; that is, each time the design loop is crisscrossed, new information is generated which propels all related fields to the next plateau. In the process of travelling up the design-manufacturing – marketing helix, the mapping between two adjacent domains begin with high level requirements. Top level design requirements are identified and conceptual design solutions are generated first. After the high level design decisions are verified, the problem is subdivided into more detailed sub-tasks and the process is repeated. According to the description, the design solution with the minimum information content can successfully satisfy design requirements with the greatest probability.

To let customers be willing to buy products with higher or the highest price, the product must have new and high performance customers need, and have good qualities, timely delivery and good service after sales. If the product is not new or high performance its price cannot be raised because of its similarity in the market. Concurrent engineering is another proven approach that can help firms to achieve shorter time to market, reduced development costs and high quality products. It requires people with different disciplines to do mapping and decomposition with the design axioms simultaneously. As for spending on product or process design, it can be reduced by using CAD and internet based design because drawing is the most time consuming and spending on it is the main part. Similarly newly designed PCBs (printed circuit boards) have gained a critical advantage because of the demands it had created like: the demand for miniaturization and weight reduction, the demand for higher data transmission rates, designing to give higher functionality and reliability, and development in component and packages and assembly technology.

High impact can be created by a successful product market strategy, how managers create and exploit market opportunities and a greater potentiality to follow a strategy of focused differentiation. All these depends on how marketing is practiced in small new business, difference in use of marketing techniques between types of firms, using marketing in small firms to improve performance and successfully managing the key issues involved in small business growth and development. It is said that market share always helps profitability. But sometimes it is found that high level of new products damage profits in high growth markets, this is when a balance between production, economic growth, competition of firms, similarity of products and businesses, cost structure and utilizing new technology has to be carried out, which is a very vast study. Moreover in slow growth markets, value is more important and i.e utilizing the idea of creating this value that domestic firms can learn from . But there is always a serious adoptability gap that makes the individualistic firm a value leader. High growth markets often require a deterministic model for future capacity needs. There is always a value added impact on ROI in slow growth countries that can be more modified by bringing idea for co-creation and using economy competence.

E-commerce is also an high impact business. There are many barriers to e-commerce adoption which can be as high cost of e-commerce implementation where the small business should think of using different activities. It is also too complex to implement its processes. Small businesses have a narrow product/service range and a limited share of market and therefore heavily rely on few customers, they are product oriented whereas large businesses are more customer oriented. They are not interested in large shares of the market and are unable to compete with their large counterparts. Small businesses have lower control over their external environment than large businesses, thus experts should be brought to do the job. Companies are well aware of a corporate strategy which were frequently professionally managed: It consists of the opportunity cost of management time. The discrepancy between business-specific knowledge and focus on individual business managers and that of corporate parents. Mistakes in reading or in sending signals. All these problems can be solved when these problems are systematically overcome. The e-commerce strategies are applied after the problem is solved.

Business network is also an important way of providing value to a business where the relationship of a business with its suppliers, customers and with other businesses in the same industry has to be defined and the basic way of understanding the linkage helps in providing the basic idea for co-operation. Companies have interdependencies among each other. These interdependencies form on basis of need for technology training in one company and another company's ability to provide it or the need for agreements regarding producing or purchasing. Another possibility is sharing intellectual property rights. Another reason for co-operating to provide an impact is to develop a strategic network more than any other form of alliance is the high level of opportunity to add value between the two companies, by ensuring that they reach the market before their customers. Analysis of data and forming pie-charts, bar graphs , questionnaires that show the effectiveness and ideas is another form of showing and considering a high impact business. An acute advantage in this is through written information or personal contacts, as well as Google scholar, BNET and many other e-learning and blogging sites provide a key advantage.

Core operations and high technology ventures are very important. Once the base business's technology and market strengths and weaknesses have been carefully analyzed, the same process must be undertaken for proposed high-technology ventures. The management team leading a charge into unfamiliar high-technology venture plunges into an acquisition or investment program without first determining the key factors that will determine success in the new target markets it plans to enter. The level of technological sophistication required by a new business is always underestimated. In many cases the specific technologies and other factors critical to success are never identified. Large investments in advanced technology are sometimes thereby wasted. Managements ability to identify critical technology links between core businesses and new ventures can be seriously impaired without such an understanding. Even though technology may be required, it may be possible to leverage entry into the new market based on usage of key resources from the core business. For these reasons it is essential that the startup phase of a repositioning drive include a critical-success factor analysis of both new ventures and core businesses. The need for analysis of the core business may come as a surprise. Strong performers in an industry often do not fully comprehend the basis of their success. Yet a strategic repositioning program virtually always requires either changes in the firm's approach to its core business or redeployment of resources out of the core business to build the new business. These may include changes in investment levels or use of the base business's technologies or market resources to support the new business. There are different management parameters that are important which are as managing the levels of the following principles: planning intensity(that would undermine the level, need, requirement, intention and administrative ability to do any planning process), after that comes the product life cycle(the greatest impact is created when the product is better managed, has higher needs, has very less of prototypes and has planned a future capacity and capability.), after that comes people intensity(that measures the strength and adoptive ability of the employees as well as the people concerned), need for differentiated compensation(it is a step that comes after people intensity and is mainly created to manage the requirements from people and ability of people as well as different award, recognition, value creation and different other HR rules), after that comes need for performance criteria consistency that would determine(the basis like benchmarking and adopting the different measuring and controlling tools to bring in the impact). The final part is compensation variability , that would determine the process and creative conscience of productive ability that would bring in the need for compensation. There are also few other major rules for creating an impact business, which can be termed as long term horizons that should be planned through econometrics or statistical forecasting , keeping that to be another tool other than data analysis. Marketing skills also provide a main set for argument that would lead to understanding the main relevance for helping to win targets. It is necessary to counteract the genuine group pressure and impact of the experience on owner managers who are able to understand how the market is opposed. Customer value attributes, creative problem solving analysis that consists of(mind mapping, clustering, selection etc) as well as understanding the product category can favorably influence business processes and the important customer needs to be met.

In the past few years, executives in charge of business clusters based upon shared production processes have become acutely aware of the need to plan for these various product market combinations as a set. It had been discovered that it is not possible to write a strategic plan or even a sales plan for individual product market combinations. The ability to offer products to one market depends upon commitments made to other markets. There is after all a common production source. One cannot justify a grow share or a exit strategy for a particular product market combination without taking into account the impact of that strategy on work stations within the plant and on the customers reaction to a decision to drop products from the line. To measure and to reach the fulfillment of the core business prospects the research centre or the technology centre should be able to market the current state of its central technology and take this core technology to a future state, as well as maximize the past investment. Clusters become more obvious to help in this formation and is possible only after it has been defined and power is required to establish this business cluster. Clusters bring the ability to benefit other firms from core technology and if this technology is too futurist, then clusters become powerful.

Globalization is also a key area to deal with and globalization very often carries the major challenges for development of SMEs through global orientation, economic competitiveness, technology improvements and policy initiatives. Apart from the globalization model, communications model is another important area to look upon. It consists of organizational objectives, which leads to conglomerate system communication model consisting of the key drivers like consultation, collaboration and cooperation which leads to the subsystem business communication strategy which shows and derives the effectiveness and the behavioral impacts of a business.

There are different group of innovators like high innovators, medium innovators and low innovators. High innovators are more likely to believe that being innovative is more important than being efficient than either the medium or low innovators. High innovators have benchmarked at a mean of 2.44 which is which is more than twice more than low and medium innovators. High innovators encourage co-operation over a competitive relationship between parts of their business than medium innovators. High innovators help in developing competitiveness through information technology and have a highly skilled administrative force and improves their production methods every financial year. High innovators have a better degree of market control and finds market newness than low or medium innovators.

HIGH GROWTH MARKETS – IMPACT OF NEW PRODUCTS

PRODUCTION AND OPERATIONS	ECONOMIC GROWTH	COMPETETITION OF FIRMS	SIMILARITY OF PRODUCTS AND BUSINESSES	COST STRUCTURE	UTILIZING NEW TECHNOLOGY	COMPETENCE & CAPACITY
- Immense Production Capacity - Operation seems to spread with strategic locations	- High growth depends on exploitation of Market Capability and Environment - Economy has high preference on the Product- Economy cope up ability of Firms.	- Firms compete with less emphasis on similar products but on creativity and ability to produce and its measurements	- Similar products can not get a huge chunk of a high growth market. - It makes it stagnant and (crunch). The economy collapses (looking at self-exploitation purpose)	- Cost is some times depended on technology more than sales or brand image. -Idea brings the cost structure	- New technology creates higher value that has to be more research producing to utilize it fully. - New technology should be able to identify key requirements	- Competence understanding for further growth and increasing contributions is very important. - It is very important to understand the core competence of products through proto types

B. CHATTERJEE (2009)

In a recent exploitation of the new technology market in the UK, it has been found that new technology based businesses will tend to employ large number of R&D personnel, as well as highly qualified staff in other functions and direct a high proportion of expenditure on R&D. As the market becomes more tangible and grows, various selection processes such as customer preference tend to favor one specification, and eventually a dominant design emerges. At this stage competitive advantage is likely to shift to those businesses that can efficiently produce large volumes of what will generally have become a commodity product. It is clear that these innovative sectors would experience rapid advances in technology which generates new opportunities for which there would be no extant market, whilst production technology would tend to be changing. There are many uncertainties in innovation of new technologies where the customer segments that would be most profitable, this being affected by segments propensity to adopt new products, the value that would attribute to the products, the overflow effects on other segments and the longer term development of demand within such segments. This seems to be a very complicated uncertainty related to new product and technology development.

Small businesses are seriously identified as disruptive technology business .Moreover other businesses are also possible to cultivate upon and consist of leadership and processes whose data can be earned through an internal department questionnaire that rightly guesses the internal environment and its requirements. Its subparts that create a high impact business through effective business results are people management, policy and strategy, resources, people satisfaction, customer satisfaction and impact on society. In order to meet the strategic requirement of an e-business or create a sufficiently strong impact business. The firm has to: acquire e-business competence by establishing partnerships for outsourcing work on design, development and execution of an e-business plan and its associated technologies. Explore new channel through internet applications would be the only left opportunity in marketing channels. Look at value proposition of the channel and SCM and CRM.

Moreover successful small businesses have many pro-growth criterias that create a major challenge to business like supporting and challenging established assumptions and paradigms. Activating prior knowledge, utilizing cognitive tools, enabling socialized learning, exposure to cross-sector and global best practices. The other personal attributes of a successful business are something that pools and utilizes internal firm specific, and network addressable assets and evolution through tacit and explicit information exchange. There are also many measurable business performance outputs, which are as explaining the uncertainties in measuring management, strategic control through entrepreneurial units, achievement of collective learning and efficiency and increased market knowledge and orientation, to search for market newness. Achievement is also based through ethical competencies and dealing with paradox and contradiction in the external environment. It is an utmost importance to highly valuing, logical and rational thinking, along with that of lateral and creative thinking nature and the need to source employees with a balanced mix of these capabilities.

Theodore Levitt once said that almost anything can be differentiated. Thus very genuinely a value map can be derived that would show a quality description with price on basis of economy, average and premium based on relative price and relative quality. On the two sides are the value proposition that would show whether the firm or its core product would grow and prosper or wither and die. Another measure that can be formed is the significance of market differentation that keeps track of performance difference among competing suppliers on key product and service attributes. In markets where performance does differ among competitors, a winning business will achieve a perceived quality advantage while others would wind up with low quality scores. A graph with market differentiation and relative quality consists of specialty products in the middle which have high impact from niche products and power of market segmentation, segmentation ideas and production and pricing qualities that would drive the product forward. The impact can be differentiated into inferior, superior or weak and strong.

STRATA 1	STRATA 2	STRATA 3	STRATA 4	STRATA 5	STRATA 6
Competition based upon Capacity	Competition based upon Size	Competition based upon Reliability	Competition based upon Price	Competition based upon Location	Competition based upon Retention
- Market need in established Market - Prototype Study - Design benefits and look at mass market, niche market and continuous production capability - Reduction of inventory	- Market strength Power of Market - Established markets, New markets -Comparison with emerging markets. -Product use customer base - Market trends.	- Market potential To value the disruptive technology. - Source and information that helps in understanding the value - Study the value gap that creates product recreation	- Pricing decisions based on: * Performance * Reliability * Previous factors * Focus * Market analysis * Price comparison * Value curve	- Locational measures to understand logistics support. - Distance from firms in clusters. - Distance between buyers and sellers - GIS, Competition for logistics performance	- Product – knowledge, nature of product. - Other products - Different models. - Product use - Performance measurement using balanced score card

B.Chatterjee (2009)

Impact businesses can be derived in different dimensions and the first categorization is in emphasis on value and commodity provider efficiency to its effectiveness. Second dimension leads to understanding the effort given to the impact created which is a measurement of total utilization of the resources or effort equal to manpower strength and ability given. Third motivational force is working with all companies to targeting companies. The fourth dimension deals with making an analysis as to the ability of the salesforce and the model this salesforce has to create to penetrate different markets and reach sufficient suppliers. The fifth step looks at working with different businesses to construct businesses that trade together. The last step deals with working together to improve the capability, by using different management functional techniques. The higher impact on larger firms can be generated through risk categorization consisting of processes like purchasing, customer risk, project risk, fiscal risk, contingency, reputation, passivity and many other different processes and sub-processes that forge the idea of dynamic own practices through consulting data that forms the major output. These risks may be external and internal and consists of various processes starting from events, business processes, positioning and liabilities. New product innovation is undefined and it is not only risk that affects it, but new products for markets as yet undefined and undimensional, new products for an established market, new products for the currently served markets and new product extensions. These are the relational measures between new product innovation, risk and impact businesses.

There are often few process activities like resource control that are involved which consist of discussion of customer needs, assess feasibility of configuration to the customers specifications, refer to list of available options outside standard configuration, discuss modifications with internal experts. Resource control consists of understanding customer needs to consideration of customer request to updating information systems with new knowledge. It is very important to collect information in dialogue with the customer in its requirements. There are also other aims to decision centres like routing customer enquiries to the relevant experts in the company, initiating new product development and assigning resources to the consideration of customer requests. Autonomous decision-making by product specialists with collaborative support from other functions as well as designing a product model structure across each product type and reinventing the process for effective CRM is another function. Thus businesses are adopting product configuration through human expertise in decision making and competitive bidding.

It can be concluded that higher impact can be provided with the speeds in time to market that reduces technological obsolescence , provide early warning of potential business disruption, mitigating the bureaucracy of strategic planning process and accommodating the increasing speed and complexity of business that can become unmanageable with traditional planning cycle. The technology driven business strategy process consists of discovery based, recognize inherent uncertainty and incorporate uncertainty resolution, be iterative, focus on the different customer and market perspectives and future orientation. It needs to be dynamic and collaborative to resolve the uncertainty and learning opportunities not only the traditional focus but also the developments made in this chapter.

Chapter 11

(Baisham Chatterjee student UNBSJ)
Modern implications on Research and development

The research expertise starts with a very broad objective which consists of concrete experiences, testing implications of concepts in new situations, formation of abstract concepts and generalizations and observation and reflections. All these are the virtual and preliminary perspectives that leads to the very broad idea of R&D. Research is a possible idea of analyzing, devising and implementing a particular problem. When a research framework is prepared it generally looks at leading and supporting quality research by implementing best practices. A clear research strategy linked to national priorities and a systems in place to investigate complaints and deal with irregular or inappropriate behavior in the conduct of research. There should be a research governance framework with national standards and its effective management through learning networks and training.

For a successful new product there are a lot of activities and information system involved which consist of management that is a thorough inclusion of authority, support, technical aspects and communication. Process consists of timing, pre-development activities, development activities, marketing activities and launch activities. Other aspects involved are company, people (their quality including being a product champion), strategy that consists of synergy and describing product characteristics and even information. The research planning can be finalized but there should also be an intense coordination between marketing and R&D for new product development. R&D and marketing integration provide a model for determining the level of integration by considering organizational strategies, environmental uncertainty and organizational factors. It is said that integrated technology would be the new process of research and development.

Researchers at Toshiba have developed a new material as part of the company's core research program in nanotechnology. It helps in producing films of material that are one billionth of a metre in dimension. It helps in production of a film of material that has an energy consumption that is only a fraction of that used by our existing plasma or LCD displays. These are great inventions that shades a light of moving away from prototypes.

After configuring the basics it is important to look at value proposition that looks at differentiation, fast time-to-market and disruptive innovations. In addition differentiation can also be done by VOC or voice of customer process. This process can be carried out better in the later stage when the customer sees and uses a prototype. In addition, rapid cycles of brainstorming, concept development, prototyping and customer feedback catalyze a more rapid R&D innovation cycle. Testing concepts, designs and ideas along the development process speeds up the learning curve and allows designers to come up more easily with an innovative offering. R&D offers explosive growth that requires new technologies or core competencies, ideas that would be more ideal to those who are not the company's best customers, find out different sales channel and should not be evaluated using a net present value analysis. Thus concepts between these three above aspects can be brought closer by increasing more focus on values and more rigid focused SMEs.

Many large companies are not short of new product ideas-the problem lies in deciding in which ones to invest substantial sums of money and then justifying these decision to senior managers. Thus it is possible to see why market research is so frequently used without hesitation, as decisions can be justified and defended. Small companies in general and small single product companies in particular are in a different situation. Very often new product ideas are scarce; hence, such companies frequently support ideas based upon their intuition and personal knowledge of the product. In competitive, technology-intensive industries, success is achieved with discontinuous product innovations through the creation of entirely new products and businesses, whereas product lines and extensions and incremental improvements are necessary for maintaining leadership. This is only after leadership has been established through a discontinuous product innovation. This argument is difficult to sustain on close examination of the evidence. Approaching a technology push approach to product innovation helps in targeting and control premium market segments, establish its technology as the industry standard, build a favorable market reputation, determine the industry's future evolution and achieve high profits. It can become a centerpiece in a companys strategy for market leadership. It is costly and risky. Such an approach requires a company to develop and commercialise an emerging technology in pursuit of growth and profits. It is very necessary to learn from different rules like learning from lead users, hindering the growth of innovative new products. Other ideas are market research unhelpful and the market research unable to warn of potential difficulties with the new product.

There are many purposes to effective R&D: motivating personnel, monitoring activities in progress, valuating projects profitability, selecting investment projects and areas, improving R&D effectiveness, improving communication and coordination, reducing uncertainty and stimulating learning.

There are different dimensions of performance like financial performance and innovative capability. Performance is measured in various ways which consists of setting performance targets at the individual level which are defined jointly by researchers, the project manager and the departmental head. They actively take part in performance measurement which are defined jointly by project managers.

These days the traditional ways to organize and work in industrial firms seems to become rapidly obsolete. There is a lot of talk about the new economy- where tangible, technological assets are no longer the primary foundation for competition and or building a firm. Intellectual phenomenon is a rising example. Knowledge intensive firms or firms that view their value or products and services on knowledge of their employees and external factors. New information technologies are arising every day that make entirely new ways of working and organizing possible. Traditional boundaries of time, space and communication no longer exist because of information and communication technologies, which challenges traditional ideas of leadership and management. The different activities that help the progress in designing are organized in 4 phases: conceptual phase, system level designs phase, detail design phase and testing phase. As designed in traditional models it is difficult for designers and engineering to understand the overall effects of their efforts in designing and developing products on, like assembly or manufacturing of the product designed. There are several means of understanding how development influences internal costs are available, ranging from metaphors, use cases and scenarios to prototypes end examples. Similarly design for X-approaches have attempted to create this integration by means of design tools from one perspective at a time. There needs to be a research methodology where technical problems, training/education, framing i.e helping to understand, plan, pertinent new knowledge gathering, understanding the idea towards transforming towards multiple product developments, setting expectations, providing feedback and identifying important learning points are the key resources.

The SPI is a system that is used in software development projects. In the SPI project there was an industry-related mission together with a set of research goals. There was an ambition to improve practices in each of the participating organizations and at the same time to add to the body of knowledge within the systems development profession. Collaborative practice research is in this way constantly confronted with dilemmas between practice driven and research driven goals and between general and specific knowledge interests. SPI effort is both demanding and both exciting to the researchers were often encouraged to engage themselves in the practical struggle to make things happen and succeed in the four software organizations. These goals are termed as a type of knowledge that research initiative intends to create to solve specific industrial problems and to add to the body of knowledge within the systems development profession. To bring this out into practice; this factor has to be engaged in different forms of social and technical intervention that would bring the insights into the barriers to and enablers of systems development improvement program. SPI helps to interpret the situation in which they find themselves; they must develop what-if scenarios, plans and designs to reflect on opportunities for action which brings a balance in the satisfactory work situations and develop useful solutions. An SPI project suggest that it is useful to base the overall collaboration between researchers and practitioners on a full learning cycle of understanding, supporting and improving practice. To start with the basis of the SPI consists of plenary, research forum and local research group that can be converted in to national network. All these together can be transformed in to the SPI group that are adjoined and interconnected to steering committee and local research group that together works very well to bring out the improvement project.

The strategic dimension can be formed as a consisting component of ownership, objective, organizations and outcomes that help in developing research. Even if everything works out together, it can be found that the level of achievement that is anticipated in relation to research may range from participation in the national arena to acknowledged excellence in international networks. The key organizational issues comprise of the most advanced issues to deal with. These issues relate to financial management in a context in which most income is on a project related basis. Establishing a continuing income stream and some stability of relationships with research councils and other organizations from which research funding in available. It is important to create avenues for internal and external resources, which is only possible by creating a research and information infrastructure. This infrastructure management helps in retaining staff that provides them with the idea for taking initiative and creating a research culture.

Similarly the self-assessment and benchmarking approach are focused on three major areas, that relate to the intra-firm and inter-firm comparison of practices and performance that can be balanced in different ways: guidance to participants in self-assessment and benchmarking in the area of product development, help participating firms to explore practice, receive feedback and debate choices. It is also important to help participants to develop plans to address performance limiting practices. It is also very important to understand research findings and case studies of product development projects. Product development can be formed in terms of core and enabling processes. These have five areas: product development; teamworking and organization; process development; market focus and transfer to manufacturing. All these can be classified into these general ways.

There are many managerial innovation ideas like: low expectation that their efforts would result in successful performance and capacity utilization and introducing the success in financial benefit decision, by starting with decreasing the price of a product. Similarly strategy formulation leads to understanding the difficulties in obtaining basic data that prevent comprehensive understanding of emerging markets. It is always important to build up a network of sales and technical staff and ideas behind collecting and recording data. It is necessary to consider the process of strategy formulation to be non-linear, incorporating frequent feedback loops between the phases of strategy analysis, development, implementation and monitoring. Strategy implementation is the last and final process that uses rational, analytical decision processes and diverting certain resources from being competitive in the high-end market. The major benefit of a strategy implementation plan is that the balance cost-driven and technology-driven cultures can help in doing this rather than substituting one another.

Creating a successful R&D has many dependants that are of three types: success factors, success barriers and the facilitators. It is very necessary to introduce a unique superior product, market knowledge and marketing efficiency as well as technical and production synergy and proficiency , which are all a part of the key successes. In developing these factors there is necessity to overcome the barriers, which stand as relieving the pressure of the market and economy of higher priced products, relative to competition. Having the success of being in a dynamic market and entering a highly competitive market rather than sharpening the focus of their product to adopt a highly niche market strategy, where you cannot find prototypes. Other important facilitators are a good product/company managerial and marketing resource specifications. Strong and effective marketing communication and product launch as well as being in a large,growing, high need market.

It is said that the technological innovation process has changed and this affects organizational and locational factors with research organizations, and in all the cases technological innovations are often the result of integration of technologies from different disciplines. Research operations within a firm embrace larger and larger ranges of technological fields. Decentralizing R&D units is a way to tap into external sources of knowledge. R&D activities are likely to be the result of an evolutionary path, from trivial technical support to manufacturing and marketing, to adaptation of products developed elsewhere, to development of products suitable for local markets. It is very necessary to understand the technological scope of the R&D activity, including the breadth (the range of technological activities encompassed within the units) and the depth (technical support, product development, applied research etc). R&D activity also helps in understanding the geographical scope of the activity, identifying the geographical mandate i.e whether the unit is assigned programs of innovation for the global or local market.

R&D requires creativity and requires the application of four control levers: diagnostic control systems, which monitor critical performance outcomes, belief systems which communicate core values, boundary systems, which are stated in negative terms of minimum standards and interactive control systems, which are formal mechanisms through which managers involve themselves regularly and personally in the decision of subordinates. The coexistence of the four levers allows the management control systems to simultaneously pursue multiple and partially contrasting objectives such as diagnosing activities and monitoring critical performance dimensions, motivating personnel and tailoring their behaviors toward the firms underlying values or encouraging communications and information sharing.

The foremost important part of innovation is knowledge management performance and strategy that consists of knowledge resources and its activities. Its enablers are IT systems, rule and motivation, supporting organization and change management. All the three operations starting from R&D value that relates to idea capture and evolution as well as characteristic of R&D task that leads to project based task and knowledge as well as R&D people that helps in matrix operation capability leads to identifying the organizational characteristics that lead to R&D assumption. The three enablers and factors that drive the idea of core knowledge start from an interconnectivity between technology contribution to business, the quality and quantity of patents created and R&D efficiency and speed. All of these being connected by a connectivity between business performance, R&D lifecycle and KM activities.

There are many classifications of R&D and their most modern emphasis is on: emphasis on linkage between customer needs and core competence, construction of architecture and capability and creation of discontinuous innovation and next generation dominant designs. The other ideas behind the 4th generation R&D are idealizing the system and network innovation model, management and R&D life cycles, emphasis on dominant designs so that the designs can overcome any predictable and assessed barriers. It is also necessary to understand the leadership of innovative researchers, global and collaborative organizations that through networks and intelligence centres can gather data to understand the benefits behind the particular collaboration. Knowledge based processing and online management are the other key processes.

There are many motivational and risk factors involved in development of ideas. The motivational factors are already ascertained and starts from technology complementarity, that strengthens basic or applied research, inimitability , creating success situations for meeting new and complex market demands and overcome vulnerable strategic position by strengthening own brand. There are also many risk factors involved like lack of control, gaining a competitor etc. Similarly communication consists of breaking down barriers and commitment and selection and evaluation of partners. After this sector the technology level of sector- in high tech sectors products are too complex to handle in-house and new technologies are frequently introduced. Thus product development alliances are always dependant on controlling the challenges that are mainly internal as well as external. The main part being motivation and risk as well as developing brand image through internal communication and internal promotional plans.

There are probably a lot of dilemmas and thoughts involved in e-entrepreneurship involved in industrially developed or developing countries that are designated in three distinct types: traditional, electronic and hybrid. Furthermore longitudinal research on e-entrepreneurship and small e-business development could potentially answer a number of pertinent questions that have eluded both researchers and practitioners. Bottom line issues, such as profitability and longevity in internet commerce are important considerations, in what some dismiss as crossover research. There are various journals with multiple research focuses. Unless the chosen research can cover a wide variety of subtopics, there is the real danger that the same methodologies would continue to generate similar empirical results. A very important but desired direction of future research would compare and contrast the impact that internet trading has on the socio-economic, cultural and political infrastructure of modern economies. The technological implications focuses on ICTs and the internet. Similarly, later research concentrated on the profitability and business applicability of internet innovations and related ICT development. To bring an ongoing digital revolution social and cultural aspects of Internet research that helps to build on the internet trading should not be neglected in favor of short –termist digital revolution. Internet trading is a well designed e-marketing tool that can lead to serious impact on a firms revenue potentiality and internet trading can identify the customer gap and thus help in building on that by brand value creation and understanding the different online learning opportunities that can create immense instant value opportunities by concentrating on the market positions that would determine the concerned results.

It is very necessary to understand the inter-firm R&D collaborations, and to look at it in a better way any collaboration that leads to buyer and supplier relationships should focus on the major models. Relationships in the European model may be based on dual or single sourcing with a strategic outlook. Develop longer –term contracts with less formalized base on service level agreements and technology and innovation focused on critical components. There should be high involvement on system and module suppliers and look at cost information and early product development stages (all this falling under the category of developing an automotive business through R&D input in different challenging economies). The Japanese economy is also different, where partnership is trusted by financial stakes and multiple functional interfaces like R&D to sales and putting major focus on long term contracting and frequent and planned information. There are different stages of decision making where product planning, concept design, pre-series design and series design are the key stages totally dependant on terms like collaborative frontloading and current sourcing practice: with lower cost at early stages but higher cost at later stages due to time and quality constraints.

There is a stringent rule of applying balanced scorecard to research. It is relating to the success of companies in their R&D activities, the other arises from the lack of consensus in their choice of the dimensions that should be included in reports prepared for the strategic management of this type of activity , as well as from the lack of alignments of the measurements of returns from their activities. The non-financial measurements related directly or indirectly to the R&D plays an extremely important role , both at the level of internal processes and at the corporate level. In companies with long cycles of product design and development, the cycle of innovation is more important than the operating cycle. The process of innovation usually requires a longer period of time for value creation, in which new markets and new customers see their expectations met. At the time of measurement of content validity the next step leads to unidimensionality, construct validity and criterion related validity which ultimately leads to final application of the scale. A internal dimension and a structure helps in reaching this idea of a successful balanced scorecard.

Mature R&D concepts are emphasized by factors like explicitation of critical knowledge, which consists of problem solving capabilities and cocreating different ideas to get it done, analyzing sociopolitical and legal appropriability conditions, R&D stage identification, relevance of research field, innovations closeness to market and explicitation of critical knowledge. The last of all are discovery assets which consists of IPR&D tested for functioning. Voluntary R&D models gives a better picture of the companys discovery intangibles. These approaches dealing with intangible assets in their entirety or focusing solely on R&D are mainly based on indicators which are supposed to reflect the economic properties of intangibles. It is based on corporate R&D that totally fit the picture.

These are the thorough output and specifications of an R&D system that can lead to project maneuvering and its increased improvement through its internal processes and different organizational development measurements , makes the R&D perform comparatively to modern R&D and changing technology by giving it a strong cohesive base to understand and develop on any related idea.

Chapter 12

(Baisham Chatterjee student UNBSJ)
Prototype management

It is to be noted that patterns are not possible to remove completely, but precisely to some extent extensive research can reduce patterning and duplicity and mainly it is small firms that start up with this idea . But prototyping starts when the R&D is established .Many firms in the modern world are increasingly relying on automated systems to improve efficiency, quality, productivity and customer satisfaction. Such systems are applied discretely that tends to reduce the operational and strategic utilities of the automation effort which is a more systemic approach. It is said that prototypes can be removed in various ways from the customers perspective that leads to order entry, inspection of the manufacturing parts and its assembly which ultimately lead to test run and assessment of the various parts and its different business activities. Manufacturing environment is another important possibility that leads to continuously entering new orders and updating old orders. Other behind for success behind removing prototypes are reviewing production status, update customer records, load new messages and print financial reports. The user layer and processing layer should have process files that can not only change the status of enquiry and storing but also manage and develop new work. It is very important to analyze tools for network planning and modeling, a simulation and design aid for switched networks etc. All these are possibilities used in telecommunications and expert system. Thus telecommunications is a very swift way of managing the different ways like expert analysis and networking which can thus reduce the prototypes brought out by other networking companies. A lot of research is on the process in Canadian telecommunications companies that can lead to building a supportive network for prototype products RIM(research in motion is an example).

ICT firms have an important phenomenon of managing prototypes. In ICT firms spreadsheet alternative that offered an economical option that appeared attractive initially, but careful consideration of the mechanics of using a spreadsheet ranked this alternative below that of customizing a prototype database. A critical aim of the model was to ensure that it summarized all of the collected information in one location without the need to re-enter data or modify it in multiple locations at a later date. Using the significance of the foremost importance improved estimates of the actual resources required to compile data. Non-financial statistics, comparison between proposed costing, reduction in implementation costs overcome barriers that hinder the effectiveness of the implementation process.

Assessing quality standards is an important way of removing duplicity. Quality manuals, quality plans and procedures that lead to understanding working instructions, modules like design, production and CRM, maintenance and calibration, quality control records module, corrective and preventive standards for any mistake in designing that would reduce or force to reduce the quality standards and at last making a management review of the total finds as an empirical access to modern prototype management. Data management is another important administrative ability that consists of evaluation, testing and identification reports that provide the major statistical framework for model management as well as provides a knowledge base for finding solutions to problems recurring from all these situations. Application software would consist of the key processes in understanding the analytical processing and information processing for quality management. Management automation is another key issue that facilitates a more structured product development process and at the same time, a more effective integration of humans and machines that reduces product development costs and cycle time while improving product quality. They can better articulate product requirements and different technical approaches. Similarly product design seldom has the opportunity to take advantage of the wealth of customer requirement information in existing product. Shortened product life cycles, expensive investments in product development and the proliferation of product varieties, the existing approaches are often constrained by the schedule deadline and lack of objectivity in defining product specifications. Comparative management, looking at key externalities, future demand trends, key production costs are the key areas that provide superiority and external belief of brand value and greatness of a product.

It is often said that teamwork enables the creativity, initiative and problem solving capabilities of people to be harnessed effectively to the potential of integrated technologies and systems. Global competition, downward pressure on costs, restructuring, downsizing, outsourcing and core employees are the major challenges that can bring the greatest asset in thinking and putting the endeavor to bring new ideas. Education through training combined with personal skills, as well as making a feedback and analysis, conceptual design in bringing out any change, making detailed design and prioritization through a gap analysis can bring things closer and make the conceptual matters more even. Gap analysis tends to bring a very suitable framework through business process and conceptual reengineering to bring the right and most correct view. Meta-planning capabilities and integration of user knowledge into the planning process. Planning procedures are reusable at any abstraction level when uniformity of the interface is met. The programmed procedures can be measured in one hand with complex abstractions. Meta –planning concept refers to support that would rectify current problems and match the detected conditions with the prediction of various tools. Thus meta-planning creates a great impact in developing the future and impact of any and all the processes of a firms business.

To bring an overall view on prototypes, core competence has to be clearly defined. It deals with identifying and categorizing the existing resources and the core competence (which can be identified by market study of new trends in technology, networking to understand what technologies other market leaders may come up with), what strategy would be required to understand potentiality and using resources to fill the current gap. All these can be brought up with strength factors and opportunity factors, which both can be arranged to fill the resource gap and customer focus, along with a step by step breakdown procedure. Core competence is a general and accepted factor today. The other factor that can reduce time-to-market and hence gain dominance is the product design collaboration over the internet which can create a competitive advantage. Integration and collaboration are a common term in the enterprise system. In collaborative product design, the different expertise systems can contribute with domains of expertise at various stages to overcome the major weakness of traditional face-to-face collaboration. However, current workflow management technologies have difficulties in solving the challenges of collaborative product design in a distributed environment with dynamic nature of product development, distributed knowledge and resources and risks attached to design collaboration. It makes the firm loose direct control over the product development process and incomplete information is disclosed with lack of transparency. Thus the two key areas of solving this problem is the RDF (resource description framework) and agent based workflow management systems(AWfMS).

There are various means of prototyping that are used, which are as rapid prototyping, that plays an essential role in product development, starting from conceptual design to final product verifications, such as aesthetic analysis, ergonomic evaluation, functional testing and process evaluation and is a more diverse way of managing prototypes. Another form of prototyping is the digital or computer generated prototyping that can reduce the ill effects of too many prototypes. Thus design is persuaded to take place as early as possible in the product life cycle because the cost of a product is set at the design stage before being spent at the manufacturing stage, so that any product changes made during the design stage should have a negligible effect on product costs. Concept design 3D and numerical controlled programs, helps in understanding the process plans and through this ideas like human factor simulation, tooling, assembly drawing can be derived. Computer integrated manufacturing strategy and computer aided engineering policy help in this to reach a goal and with the help of virtual prototyping and 3D controlled machine the product can reach different measures in productivity. There are many important pattern formations that can be recognized, which are as observed pattern sentence, that leads to the cycle that leads to template matching with cyclic pattern and compute similarity coefficient. Other factors pertaining to that are completing phase translation. All these are controlled through original algorithm and pertain more towards the observed pattern.

Kaplan and Norton has a lot of work on building on prototypes through revenue growth strategy and productivity strategy which consists of value from new products and improve asset utilization through customer intimacy all of which arise through employee competencies, technology and corporate culture. There are many ways of deriving success which are as understanding the know-how gap between the person building the prototype and the designers. It is also very important to identify a low level of technical expertise among the designers and using knowledge sharing as a key source. There is importance of fragmented outputs from different approaches and there is importance of finding difficulty of system integration. In order to understand the maintenance of different notations, gaps and mismatches in adopting different approaches have to be assumed. Electronic mail is the best possibility of understanding prototypes and describing it. New product development is an integral part of SMEs where R&D costs are a big involvement. Challenges of new product, including a new set of vendors and increased competition and rapid diffusion of technology are the key factors. Process proficiency too helps in removing patterns sometimes. Teams follow a clear plan or roadmap of measurable milestones, idea generation, screening and evaluation are other key factors.

Three dimensional prototype models can put engineering, management, manufacturing and marketers, as well as customers on an equal footing in the evaluation of a design. Prototypes provide a clarification of communication and they span distance and disciplines, such as an engine component being available to design the foundry, production and assembly, look towards discipline and experience for a better performing and look towards more appealing design or one that is more cost effective to provides. All firms deal with prototypes except those that start with genius ideas and these ideas are stable enough for the firm to deal with that for 2-3 years along with its patent rights. After that as more ideas develop prototyping starts increasing. Collaborations form an integral part, where potential users combine with systems expert to develop a combined information sourcing skills, and inform input by users all together in a user friendly system. These are all together in the form of information specialists and idea behind a developing system that together leads to idea refinement and evaluation. Information technology is often linked to actual and potential users, as well as develop initial prototype with that idea that through brainstorming and evaluation can provide a definite identity.

Rapid prototyping remains expensive on a per-part-produced basis. Hence most of the rapid prototypes are made in a carefully controlled business environments where such expense fits. Rapid prototyping might gain acceptance and grow more quickly if the technologists took on more of a business view so that they could demonstrate to management –in management terms-that rapid prototyping offer real business value that outweighs their expense. However, the benefits depend on topics that go beyond the initial procurement. Even if the developer is successful in obtaining a certain rapid prototyping capability, for instance, ultimate success will depend not only on the developers skill in applying the technology but also in the managements genuine acceptance of the technology and its implications for running the business. To definitively access a prototype model for further changes, we look at constructing a quantitative scenario which justifies whether customers might not buy the product at all if it were six months late, which would defer their purchase, market share and referrals are other ideas . Extra engineering labor may be collected during the delay period, but this labor expense has usually got the smallest effect. Pattern making and design creation are a high support for prototype creation. Only design creation can somewhat lead to more patterning and slowly the patterns may increase to such an extent that duplicity or similarity is removed completely. But that requires very high technical skills. Rapid prototyping is a process of managing the cost effective prototypes in the modern world. However, no technology can stay successful in its stand-alone form in a dynamic and competitive global market. An approach for making rapid prototyping visual and available to everybody , it has been combined with the internet.

The background and its importance to understand the benchmarking procedures, as well as focus groups, preliminary designs. After that comes the personal interviews, then final designs and then final product analysis. These together bring the idea of rapid prototyping allowed for the physical realization of desirable features, aesthetic designs and ergonomic design factors. In different design evaluations, the relationship between the mechanical package, printed circuit board and other electronic components. A more useful form of virtual prototype in the context of product development, is one that tells the user how it will perform and behave in its intended environment. It is thought that computing technology is another form of immersive technology, leaving aside the problems of moving towards immersive environments. Analytical virtual prototypes will not be used efficiently within the product development process until geometric representations are efficiently integrated with analysis applications. Designers & customers with the help of presentation, product data generation and evaluation and aid of product model, process model and activity model can simulate the environment that can help in manufacturing and production management. Innovation and competition together create the major thrust for change. A very diverse idea can stay for a long time, but prototyping can increase a products sales life cycle, the rapid to market company gains a pricing advantage and can help in creating up to date technology and market advantage. There should also be fixed cost for product development through early release and reduction of project overhead and help in the ability to delay design commitments. Cost of design and cost of typing and formation of the design are very important. Thus it is very important that product design and analysis should go hand in hand with new ideas. It is not necessary that prototypes are necessary to be kept, but so to run businesses in emerging markets. But when someone looks only towards creating management models and charts or look at fields like biogenetical engineering or fields in geologistical services things are different and need to have a very creative focus, and it is not necessary that all its services would have patterns.

Conclusion

This book consists of ideas that are self created and designed in different sequences that match the idea of modern technology development. All the diagrams are self-created and measures the innovation change and the modern innovation paradigms accurately. There has been a lot of instances on the basic mindset of the innovation and the basics of innovation that would provide the key economics factors that would bring out the complexity of innovation and creativity. Very often it is found that innovation has barriers but sometimes thinking wisely innovation has no boundaries or has immense creativity in a particular region. The few chapters in this book are dependant on the general factors that are dependant on the innovative capability of North America. Sometimes it is found that the value curve that gives further emphasis on the industry standard and creates a market space for the required amount of scope of the product and service offering helps in describing the potentiality of a firm and its pursuit to innovate further. The best innovators use old ideas according to market trends as well as use product development teams to create breakthroughs, that would create incremental improvements and finally a breakthrough for profit. Businesses that constantly innovate have systematized the production and testing of new ideas, a strategy that authors called knowledge brokering. It is important to make a high degree of legal and resource protection and help in understanding the cost target. As things become more mature, its abilities stern from its processes- product development, manufacturing and budgeting. It is found that logistics, development, manufacturing or customer service are more likely to be the less visible background processes that support decisions about where to invest resources- those that define how market research is habitually done and how much analysis is translated into financial projections. There are many pros and cons of disruptive and sustainable technologies where no companies depend on customers and investors for resources as well as small markets don't solve the growth needs of large companies and finding new markets and having the ability to bring change in existing markets is a key paradigm. It is very important to ascertain organizations capabilities and technology supply that creates market demand. Sustaining technological development helps develop insurmountable advantages in manufacturing costs and design experience, and they eventually withdrew from the market. But very often product design, manufacturing and marketing create the greatest impact in developing the creative base of a firm that brings the key potentiality in growth of a firm. It is very natural that entrants grow and improve, but sometimes entrants find barriers in the impact they might create because of the nature of their competitors.

There are many innovative practices like high cost of developing significant improved products or processes and qualifying for government assistantship programs which helps in accessing expertise in universities. I have also focused more often on R&D capabilities and technological competence as well as modern technological capabilities and ideas that would lead to bringing out the core concepts that help in developing R&D concepts in North America and Europe. Very often it is found that R&D capability is located in a single country or has a single production base that can help in wider joint and conglomerate ideas to create a breakthrough point for medium sized companies. Large companies carry a high networking base in other countries that create huge marketing expertise through a very sustainable R&D. It is mainly the ICT firms that carries knowledge and ideas even to distant countries in South East Asia. Chemical firms, as well as pharma majors show a great competitive advantage in exploiting those markets. R&D is probably a very noteworthy phenomenon that can be exploited by understanding and correctly determining the competitive force, market size and ability of the market to force ideas or build up ideas and products that would fit the market now or in future. R&D is the most talked about thing that can bring changes and developments in completely anything. R&D can also be created in house by a group of minds or a single mind working together by exploiting the major challenges or factors that enable the development of a part of the economy or an opportunity. Thus R&D can be termed as the basic mindset of innovation or something to start with.

There are many ideas behind locational theory and improving performance. Cost reduction and strategy implementation are the important sequences that lead to understanding the intention to manipulate and undertake the ability to sort out technical difficulties. It is often found that there are various networking problems and inability to spread innovation throughout different countries. At this point of time there should be a properly set GIS, or internet services that would help in any kind of marketing orientation or communications ability with the support of online ads and E-commerce that would penetrate even very difficult to penetrate markets. Innovation always needs certain skills starting from studying of prototypes and its use, as well as defining the idea of need and use of prototypes and improving the patterns of products manufactured by any organization. It can also be seen that emerging companies need to have a very broad spectrum of opportunities that can create a disruptive outlook. It is true that in the modern world only disruptive firms outshine other mid-sized firms and create a very respectable image in journals. There are many firms in the United States, Denmark and

Germany that have won through their disruptive base and have outshined firms in many countries in the west. It is true that disruptive firms improves the prospects of higher revenue and higher growth through more unpredictable technology base, but there is the necessity of great knowledge and highly calculative leadership to support this. Sustainable technology is often overlooked, but most of the emerging markets and developed firms are taking the help of sustainable technologies to expand the firms business and help the countrys economy grow. Technology can be drawn in various ways as in the highly complicated self-created figures, that I have produced. Indeed my work would stand out to be a great piece of achievement when it latest models on alliances, marketing and technology, disruptive technology, segmented outlook of the various aspects of technology come into view. Moreover it can be found that many ideas are sufficiently well organized to reproduce in this book with the most modern creative outlook. Moreover it can be ascertained that sometimes there is need of modern mindset and university-industry alliances and education to start a disruptive, rapid prototyping or any form of creative business that would surpass any form of functional problem from the traditional outlook that sometimes retards the firms business of puts too many competitors. Generally traditional businesses in emerging markets or sustainable technologies cover greater market gap and create much greater revenue, but this is when innovation or the basic mindset comes into play . The basic mindset of innovation provides a much broader outlook than the traditional thoughts and hence this is the first chapter that provides great importance.

Moreover chapter like continuation of disruptive technology, integrated technologies have wonderful ideas that has been brought to view. Everything is a combination of the most recent view on disruptive technology and any modern technology developments that would remove any of the imbalances that may be created. Moreover any knowledge or idea that is created in the modern world is a collection of any recent technical aspects or news and interviews. It is through years of experience that people brought out these ideas which requires a lot of expertise and ability to bring out these technologies. New technologies related to genetic engineering or disruptive technology created for finding particle counts have proved to be a key success factor. A lot of data has been collected from most of the books written by Clayton Christensen and books from theoretical perspectives in some British publications. This book consists of very creative understanding and knowledge that would enable to know the gaps and findings of innovation that would make innovation easily understandable, bringing into view the most recent innovation dilemmas. Organizational innovation and integrated technologies are the other talked about factors in the modern world. Starting from books by Marco Iansiti, Henry Chesbrough these books bring into view the most modern internal organizational management perspectives. There are many papers and books of American, European and Canadian publications from which data has been taken. Thus this book provide advantages to know about the key success factors of innovation.

References

BOOKS

1) Carol Walcoff, Robert P. Ouellette, Paul N. Cheremisinoff (1983): Techniques for managing technological innovation **Ann Arbor Science (The Butterworth Group).** 17-46,77,101-111,114,124.

2) Hariolf Grupp (1998):Foundations of the economics of innovation **Edward Elgar Publishing Ltd (UK).**49-88,99-140,301-359.

3) Christopher Freeman (1990): The economics of innovation **Edward Elgar Publishing ltd (UK).**55-66,107-151,185-248, 291-332, 396-427.

4) Harold Leavitt, Lawrence Pinfield and Eugene Webb (1975): Organizations of the future **Praeger Publishers** .54.

5) Melvin L.Greenhut (1956): Plant location in theory and in Practice **The University of North Carolina Press.** 17-31,76-83,106-122,163-177.

6) Fred Gault (2003): Understanding Innovation in Canadian Industry **McGill-Queens University Press.**67-99,231-275.

7) Clayton M.Christensen (2006): The innovators dilemma **Collins business essential.**39-115,118-158,

8) Clayton M. Christensen, Scott D.Anthony and Erik A.Roth (2004): Seeing whats next **Harvard business school press.**4-8,29-56,75-98.

9) Clayton M Christensen and Michael E.Raynor (2003): The innovators solution **Harvard Business School Press.**31-114,115-220.

PAPERS

1) Peter F. Drucker (1998),The information executives truly need, **Harvard Business Review.**3-11.

2) Robert G.Eccles (1998), The performance measurement manifesto, **Harvard Business Review.**30-36.

3) Robert S.Kaplan and David P.Norton (1998),The Balanced Scorecard- Measures that drive Performance, **Harvard Business Review.**124,138-139.

4) Robert S.Kaplan and David P.Norton (1998),Putting the Balanced Scorecard to Work, **Harvard Business Review.**148-150,154, 156,161,162

5) Robert S.Kaplan and David P.Norton (1998), Using the balanced scorecard as a strategic management system, **Harvard Business Review** .185-193,205-211.

6) W.Chan Kim and Renee Mauborgne (1998), Creating new market space, **Harvard Business Review.**7-12,14-27.

7) Eric Von Hippel, Stefan Thomke and Mary Sonnack (1998), Creating breakthroughs at 3M, **Harvard Business Review.**32-41, 44-47.

8) Andrew Hargadon and Robert I.Sutton (1998), Building an innovation factory, **Harvard Business Review.**57-69.

9) W.Chan Kim and Renee Mauborgne (1998), Knowing a winning business idea when you see one, **Harvard Business Review**.77-93.

10) Clayton M.Christensen and Michael Overdorf (1998), Meeting the challenge of disruptive change, **Harvard Business Review**.105-114.

11) Rosabeth Moss Kanter (1998), From Spare Change to real change, **Harvard Business Review**.154-157.

12) Stefan Thomke (1998), Enlightened Experimentation, **Harvard Business Review**.181-185, 197.

13) Axel Johne (1999), Successful market innovation, **European Journal of Innovation management**.7-9.

14) Angela Cottam, John Ensor and Christine Band (2001), A benchmark study of strategic commitment to innovation, **European Journal of Innovation Management**, 90-92.

15) Angel R.Martinez Lorente, Frank Dewhurst and Barrie G.Dale (1999), TQM and business innovation, **European Journal of Innovation Management**.13,14,17.

16) Brian S.Cumming (1998), Innovation overview and future challenges, **European Journal of Innovation Management**.22-24,27,28.

17) Valerie Chanal (2004), Innovation management and organizational learning: a discursive approach, **European Journal of Innovation Management** .57-60.

18) Anders Drejer (2002), Situations for innovation management: towards a contingency model, **European Journal of Innovation Management**. 6-9,12,14.

19) Mariano Nieto (2004), Basic propositions for the study of the technological innovation process in the firm, **European Journal of Innovation Management**. 315-317,318,319,320.

20) E.C.Martins and F.Terblanche (2003), Building organizational culture that stimulates creativity and innovation, **European Journal of Innovation Management**.65-68,70.

21) Glenn Hardaker (1998), An integrated approach towards product innovation in international manufacturing organizations, **European Journal of Innovation management**. 68,69,72.

22) Robert Sandberg and Andreas Werr (2003), Corporate consulting in product innovation: overcoming the barriers to utilization, **European Journal of Innovation Management**. 103-108.

23) Elizabeth Shaw, Andrew O'Loughlin and Elspeth McFadzean (2005), Corporate entrepreneurship and innovation part 2: a role-and process-based approach, **European Journal of Innovation Management**.394-398.

24) Stephen A.W.Drew (2006), Building technology foresight: using scenarios to embrace innovation, **European Journal of Innovation Management** .242-252.

25) E. Roland Andersson (2009),System group ideologue approach to innovation: scientific basis and practitioner guidelines, **European Journal of Innovation Management** 180-191.

26) Manuela Perez Perez, Angela Martinez Sanchez, Pilar De Luis Carnicer and Maria Jose Vela Jimenez

(2004),A technology acceptance model of innovation adoption: the case of teleworking, **European Journal of Innovation Management.**282-287.

27) John Man (2001),Creating innovation, **European Journal of Innovation Management.**229-232.

28) Paolo Pratali (2003), Strategic management of technological innovations in the small enterprise, **European Journal of Innovation Management.**20-24,25-29.

29) C.Brooke Dobni (2008), The DNA of innovation, **The Journal of business strategy.**44-46.

30) Rick Brown (1992), Managing the S Curves of innovation, **Journal of consumer marketing.**62-69.

31) Douglas K.Herrmann (1999), Tracking systems as a catalyst for incremental innovation, **Management decision.**787-791.

32) Amy Muller and Liisa Valikangas (2002), Extending the boundary of corporate innovation, **Strategy & leadership.**5-8.

33) Pierre Loewe and Jennifer Dominiquini (2006),Overcoming the barriers to effective innovation, **Strategy and leadership**. 25-31.

34) Robert G.Cooper (2007), The performance impact of product innovation strategies, **European Journal of marketing** .8-35.

35) Donald W.Mitchell and Carol Brucker Coles (2004), Establishing a continuing business model innovation process, **Journal of Business Strategy** .42-49.

36) Marnix Assink (2006), Inhibitors of disruptive innovation capability: a conceptual model, , European **Journal of Innovation Management**.217,219-228.

37) Robert Chapman Wood (2007), How strategic innovation really gets started, **Strategy & leadership**. 22-27.

38) Lawrence Owen, Charles Goldwasser, Kristi Choate and Amy Blitz (2008),Collaborative innovation through the extended enterprise, **Strategy & leadership**. 40-44.

39) Philip J.Rosson and Michael J.C.Martin (2007), The management of technological innovation and new product development, **Emerald Backfiles**. 6-12.

40) Nick Evans, Bill Ralston and Andrew Broderick (2009), Strategic thinking about disruptive technologies, **Strategy & leadership**. 24-30.

41) George Gregoire (2002), Imprint patterning: a novel method for producing high intensity interconnects, **Circuit World**.33-36.

42) Alberto F.Griffa (2008), A paradigm shift for inspection: complementing traditional CMM with DSSP innovation, **Sensor review**.335-340.

43) George Tovstiga and Ernest J.Fantner (2000), Implications of the dynamics of the new networked economy for e-business startups: the case of Philips' Access Point, **Internet research: Electronic Networking Applications and Policy.** 460-469.

44) Adrian Slywotzky (2004), Exploring the strategic risk frontier, **Strategy & leadership**. 12,13.

45) Saul J.Berman and Jeff Hagan (2006), How technology driven business strategy can spur innovation and growth, **Strategy & leadership**. 28-34.

46) Daniel J.Knight (2005), Three trips around the innovation track: an interview with Clayton Christensen, **Strategy & leadership**.13-18.

47) Chung-Shing Lee (2001), An analytical framework for evaluating e-commerce business models and strategies, **Internet research: Electronic Networking Applications and Policy**.350-358.

48) David W.Cravens, Nigel F.Piercy and George S.Low (2002), The innovation challenges of proactive cannibalization and discontinuous technology. **European Business Review**. 260-266.

49) Brian Low and Wesley J.Johnston (2009),The evolution of network positions in emerging and converging technologies, **Journal of Business and Industrial Marketing** .431-437.

50) Chris Bernard (2009), Cultural innovation in software design: the new impact of innovation planning methods, **Journal of Business Strategy**.59,60.

51) David C.Yen and David C.Chou (2001), Intranets for organizational innovation, **Information management & computer security**.81-85.

52) Su-Chao Chang and Ming-Shing Lee (2008), The linkage between knowledge accumulation capability and organizational innovation, **Journal of knowledge management**. 8.

53) Wann-Yih Wu, Chwan-Yi Chiang and Jeng-Sin Jiang (2002), Interrelationships between TMT management

styles and organizational innovation, **Industrial management & data systems**. 175-181.

54) Petra C.de Weerd-Nederhof, Bernice J.Pacitti, Jorge F.da Silva Gomes and Alan W.Pearson (2002), Tools for the improvement of organizational learning processes in innovation, **Journal of Workplace learning.**322-329.

55) Torbjorn Korsvold and Lone Sletbakk Ramstad (2004), A generic model for creating organizational change and innovation and building process, **Facilities**.304-308.

56) C.Brooke Dobni (2008), Measuring innovation culture in organizations. **European Journal of innovation management.**541-551.

57) Yongchuan Bao (2009),Organizational resistance to performance-enhancing technological innovations: a motivation-threat-ability framework, **Journal of business& industrial marketing**.121-124.

58) Camarero Carmen and Garrido Maria Jose (2008), The role of technological and organizational innovation in the relation between market orientation and performance in cultural organizations. **European Journal of Innovation Management** .421-427.

59) Steven A.Cavaleri and David S.Fearon (2000), Integrating organizational learning and business praxis: a case for intelligent project management. **The learning organization**.254-256.

60) H.James Harrington (1995), Continuous versus breakthrough improvement. **Business Process Re-engineering and management journal.**32-46.

61) Brian Leavy (2005), Value pioneering-how to discover your own blue ocean interview with W. Chan Kim and Renee Mauborgne. **Strategy& leadership**. 15-18.

62) Stefania Borghini (2005), Organizational creativity: breaking innovation and order to innovate. **Journal of knowledge management**.25-27.

63) Jon-Arild Johannessen (2009), A systematic approach to innovation: the interactive innovation model. **Kybernetes**.162.

64) Paul W.Hyland, Jose F.B.Gieskes and Terrence R. Sloan (2001), Occupational clusters as determinants of organizational learning in the product innovation process. **Journal of workplace learning**. 204-206.

65) Helen salavou (2008), The concept of innovativeness: should we need to focus?. **European Journal of innovation management** .35-39.

66) Walter Hivner , Shirley A.Hopkins and Willie E.Hopkins (2004), Facilitating, accelerating, and sustaining the innovation diffusion process: an epidemic modeling approach. **European Journal of innovation management.** 81-87.

67) Charlotta Windahl, Pierre Andersson, Christian Berggren and Camilla Nehler (2004), Manufacturing firms and integrated solutions: characteristics and implications, **European Journal of Innovation management.** 220-225.

68) Jochen Wirtz and Monica Tomlin (2000), Institutionalising customer-driven learning through fully integrated customer feedback systems, **Managing service quality**.207-214.

69) Maria Vakola, Yacine Rezgui and Trevor Wood-Harper (2000), The Condor business process re-engineering model. **Managerial Auditing Journal**.43-45.

70) Lars Frank (2004), Architecture for integration of distributed ERP systems and e-commerce systems. **Industrial management & data systems**.419-427.

71) Tilo Pfeifer, Wolf Reissiger and Claudia Canales (2004), Integrating six sigma with quality management systems. **TQM magazine**.242-247.

72) Mosad Zineldin (2000), Total relationship management (TRM) and total quality management (TQM). **Managerial Auditing Journal** .21-27.

73) Dirk Zupancic (2008), Towards an integrated framework of key account management. **Journal of Business & Industrial management.** 324-328.

74) J.Roland Ortt and Patrick A. van der duin (2008), The evolution of innovation management towards contextual innovation. **European Journal of Innovation management** . 524-531.

75) Mile Terziovski (2002), Achieving performance excellence through an integrated strategy of radical innovation and continuous improvement. **Measuring business excellence**. 6-10.

76) Jukka Ojasalo (2008), Management of innovation networks: a case study of different approaches. **European Journal of Innovation management**. 57-73.

77) Tommaso Buganza and Roberto Verganti (2009), Open innovation process to inbound knowledge. **European Journal of Innovation management**.311-322.

78) Dean Elmuti, Michael Abebe and Marco Nicolosi (2005), An overview of strategic alliances between universities and corporations. **The Journal of Workplace learning**. 121-127.

79) Hamieda Parker (2000), Interfirm collaboration and the new product development process. **Industrial management & data systems.** 256,257,258.

80) Hakan Linnarsson and Andreas Werr (2004), Overcoming the innovation-alliance paradox: a case study of the explorative alliance. **European Journal of Innovation management**. 49-53.

81) Frank Tian Xie and Wesley J.Johnston (2004), Strategic alliances: incorporating the impact of e-business technological innovations, **Journal of Business& industrial marketing**.210-218.

82) T.K.Das and Irene Y.He (2006), Entrepreneurial firms in search of established partners: review and recommendations. **International journal of entrepreneurial behavior & research**. 116-120.

83) Denise G.Jarratt (1998), A strategic classification of business alliances: a qualitative perspective built from a study of small and medium-sized enterprises. **Qualitative market research: an international journal.** 41-46.

84) F. Ian Stuart and David McCutcheon (1996), Sustaining strategic supplier alliances. **International journal of operation & production management**.9-12.

85) Hitoshi Mitsuhashi (2002), Uncertainty in selecting alliance partners: The three reduction mechanisms and alliance formation process. **The international journal of organizational analysis**. 112-117.

86) Ann Gignac and Steven H. Appelbaum (1997), The impact of stress on customer service representatives: a comparative study. **Journal of Workplace learning**. 21-27.

87) John Ling, Peter Starkey and Michael Weinhold (2008), ProSurf technology road map-a summary. **Circuit world**. 14-16.

88) Sandra Hogarth-Scott, Kathryn Watson and Nicholas Wilson (1996), Do small businesses have to practice marketing to survive and grow?. **Marketing intelligence& planning**. 7-13.

89) Keith Roberts (2003), What strategic investments should you make during a recession to gain competitive advantage in the recovery?. **Strategy & leadership**. 32-38.

90) Nerys Fuller-Love and Esyllt Thomas (2004), Networks in small manufacturing firms. **Journal of small business & enterprise development** 245-251.

91) William P. Sommers, Joseph Nemec Jr and John M. Harris (2007), Repositioning with technology: making it work. **Journal of business strategy.** 18-22.

92) Malcolm Robert Victor Goodman (1999), The pursuit of value through qualitative research. **Qualitative market research: an international journal**. 112-119.

93) Fahri Karakaya and Cem Canel (1998), Underlying dimensions of business location decisions. **Industrial management & data systems**. 325-328.

94) Damian Hine and Neal Ryan (1999), Small service firms-creating value through innovation. **Managing service quality.** 415-420.

95) Sandy Hewitt (1997), Business excellence: does it work for small companies?. **The TQM Magazine.**77,80.

96) Jennifer Rowley (2002), Synergy & strategy in E-business. **Marketing Intelligence & planning.** 217-219.

97) Bradley T.Gale and Robert D.Buzzell (2007), Market perceived quality: key strategic concept. **Planning Review.**7-12.

98) Ananda Mukherji (2002), The evolution of information systems : their impact on organizations and structures. **Management Decision.**500-503.

99) John Sparrow (1999), Using qualitative research to establish SME support needs. **Qualitative Market research: An international journal.** 121-129.

100) Jo Bramham, Bart MacCarthy and Jane Guinery (2004), Managing product variety in quotation processes. **Journal of manufacturing technology management.** 415-420.

101) Yair Holtzman (2008), Innovation in research and development: tool of strategic growth. **Journal of management development.** 1041-1048.

102) Paul Trott (2001), The role of market research in the development of discontinuous new products. **European Journal of Innovation management.**118-121.

103) Vittorio Chiesa , Federico Frattini, Valentina Lazzarotti and Raffaella Manzini (2009), Performance measurement of research and development activities. **European Journal of Innovation management.**28-31,34.

104) Jennifer Rowley (1999), Developing research capacity: the second step. **International Journal of Educational management.** 209-211.

105) Paul Coughlan and Emer Brady (1995), Self-assessment and benchmarking product development in five Irish firms. **Journal of Managerial Psychology.**42-46.

106) Vittorio Chiesa (1996), Evolutionary patterns in international research and development. **Integrated manufacturing systems.** 5-8, 12,13.

107) Pamela E.Regan and Brian H.Kliener (1997), New developments in improving quality management in research and development. **Aircraft engineering and aerospace technology.** 27-29.

108) Maria Elmquist, Tobias Fredberg and Susanne Ollila (2009), Exploring the field of open innovation. **European Journal of Innovation management.**328-337.

109) Francisco J.Cantu, Alberto Bustani, Arturo Molina and Hector Moreira (2009), A knowledge- based development model: the research chair strategy. **Journal of knowledge management.** 157-165.

110) R. William Maule (2000), Metacognitive research and development(MRDF) for internet instructional science software. **Internet research: Electronic networking Applications and Policy.**332-337,343.

111) Eric Brun, Alf Steinar Saetre and Martin Gjelsvik (2009), Classification of ambiguity in new product development projects. **European Journal of Innovation management.**65,71-75.

112) Teresa Garcia-Valderrama, Eva Mulero-Mendigorri and Daniel Revuelta- Bordoy (2008), A Balanced Scorecard framework for R&D. **European Journal of Innovation management.** 243-248, 251-266,271-273.

113) Jianxin Jiao and Mitchell M.Tseng (1999), A requirement management database system for product definition, **Integrated Manufacturing systems.** 147-151.

114) David Transfield, Ivor Parry, Sarah Wilson, Stuart Smith and Morris Foster (1998), Teamworked organizational engineering: getting the most out of teamworking. **Management Decision.**383.

115) S.H.Choi and A.M.M.Chan (2002), A dexel-based virtual prototyping system for product development. **Rapid Prototyping Journal.**304,305.

116) G.R.Bennett (1997), The application of virtual prototyping in the development of complex aerospace products. **Aircraft Engineering and Aerospace Technology.**20,23.

117) Carla van den Berg and Ioana Popescu (2005), An experience in knowledge mapping. **Journal of knowledge management.**126,127.

118) Denise Oh (1995), The role of prototyping in a bottom-up approach to systems development: the ideal. **Campus-Wide Information Systems.**13,14,17.

119) Preston G.Smith (1999), The business of rapid prototyping. **Rapid Prototyping Journal.**181,183.

120) Mitchell M.Tseng, Jianxin Jiao and Chuan-Jun Su (1998), Virtual prototyping for customized product development. **Integrated Manufacturing Systems.**335-337,380,340.

121) James E.Folkstead and Russell L.Johnson (2002), Integrated rapid prototyping and rapid tooling (IRPRT). **Integrated Manufacturing System**.98-101.

www.ingramcontent.com/pod-product-compliance
Lightning Source LLC
Chambersburg PA
CBHW032018170526
45157CB00002B/758